An Argument on Rhetorical Style

An Argument on Rhetorical Style

By Marie Lund

Aarhus University Press |

An Argument on Rhetorical Style

Cover: Carl-H. K. Zakrisson
Layout and typesetting: Anette Ryevad, Ryevad Grafisk
Publishing Editor: Henrik Jensen
This book is typeset in Adobe Garamond Pro and Trajan Pro
and printed on 100g Munken Premium Cream 13
Printed by Narayana Press, Denmark

Printed in Denmark 2017

ISBN 978 87 7184 220 3

Aarhus University Press
Finlandsgade 29
DK-8200 Aarhus N
Denmark
www.unipress.dk

Published with the financial support of Aarhus University Research Foundation

International distributors:
Gazelle Book Services Ltd.
White Cross Mills
Hightown, Lancaster, LA1 4XS
United Kingdom
www.gazellebookservices.co.uk

ISD
70 Enterprise Drive, Suite 2
Bristol, CT 06010
USA
www.isdistribution.com

MIX
Paper from responsible sources
FSC® C010651

PEER REVIEWED

/ In accordance with requirements of the Danish Ministry of Higher Education and Science, the certification means that a PhD level peer has made a written assessment justifying this book's scientific quality.

TABLE OF CONTENTS

INTRODUCTION

Style is not exactly a term reserved for the few. Most textbooks on written and oral communication contain sections on style and stylistics, and often they are based directly on Classical rhetorical theories. Today, style and stylistics are still part of the basic vocabulary of the rhetorical critic, teacher, and thinker. As a rhetorical concept, style refers to a way of using language. It distinguishes itself as being formal, but also as having consequences at the level of meaning. While style and stylistics have traditionally been linked primarily to linguistic utterances and the way in which one speaks or writes, the term *style* is also used in regards to cultural and social codes for such different areas as bodily gestures, clothing combinations, patterns of consumption, and cultural habits and references. With such a broad scope of application, the analytical potential of style ought to be enormous. However, it is also a rather slippery term that has yet to be defined unambiguously. Thus, despite having spread into different academic subjects as well as everyday language, no clearly defined research field has emerged around style as a concept.

The definition and meaning of style are important themes in *An Argument on Rhetorical Style*, but the perspective of the study can be more narrowly defined as rhetorical, in that the book focuses in particular on rhetorical issues such as strategic possibilities, argumentation, topics, deliberation, audience construction, political discourse, the impact of discursive habits on culture and society, and norms for public communication.

Style in Modern and Postmodern Rhetorical Criticism

Modern rhetorical criticism has not been heavily invested in the development of style. The modern rehabilitation of rhetoric was largely aimed at rediscovering the theory of argumentation that had been an important part of Classical rhetoric, but had since lost its status. In the last half of the twentieth century rhetoric developed as an academic discipline, which dealt with concepts like the rhetorical situation, audience, genre, and argumentation. In this important, foundation-laying phase of the academic discipline, style did not become an object of independent interest to any great extent. As a consequence of the lack of conceptual development, style is – compared to, for instance, argumentation or genre – a more loosely defined field of study. No real common theoretical approach has emerged to redefine style in a modern critical context, and research on style is therefore influenced by many apparently arbitrary theoretical connections and aims.

Modern rhetorical theories developed in the wake of World War II place rhetoric within an Enlightenment tradition. The Belgian rhetorical theorists Chaïm Perelman and Lucie Olbrechts-Tyteca define rhetoric as argumentation based on a meeting of minds, in their work *Traité de l'argumentation. La Nouvelle Rhétorique* (1958), and in so doing create a counter-image to the reputation of rhetoric as the empty art of persuasion and external decoration. Their thoughts about the common grounds of argumentation and an abstract norm for rational argumentation – the universal audience – is in line with the societal ideals for communication later developed in German sociologist Jürgen Habermas' theories of rational public discussion. In the modern rehabilitation of the rhetorical project, in which rhetoric is founded on argumentation and is placed within an ethical normative framework, the qualities of style are not immediately essential. In this respect, because it is connected to formal linguistic aspects or to aesthetic categories like feelings and senses, style sets an agenda that is secondary to political argumentation and democratic deliberation within a modernist and rationalist horizon.

The influence of thoughts and theories that may on a general basis be defined as postmodern, however, presents different challenges to the modernist, new rhetorical interpretation of rhetoric. Postmodern and poststructuralist theories criticize the view of language as representative, and as a result, the more instrumental models of communication are being revised. Under this influence, components of a more traditional rhetorical model of communication are reinterpreted as discursive phenomena that are not excluded from the rhetorical approach. Central conceptual categories like a speech, the audience, and the rhetorical situation are thus being revisited and further developed in this light. Thus, an instrumental view of rhetoric as an autonomous strategic action intended to influence an – again – autonomous audience has been problematized.

A resurgence of interest in style is a clear result of the 'discursive turn' of the theories that may be categorized as poststructuralist. While the modern, new rhetorical rehabilitation of rhetoric subordinated style to argumentation and the goal of argumentation, no simple reversal of this hierarchical relation has occurred in the style studies published in the last two or three decades. Rather, recent style studies are based on the premise of deconstructing the contradistinction between such categorizations of form and content – such as style being opposed to argumentation. These studies instead strive to examine the meaning and argumentation that style generates. With the theoretical rejection of fixed points outside language, discourse and style are established as the basis for the formation of argumentation and meaning.

Dialogue between Research Traditions

An Argument on Rhetorical Style aims to establish a concept of rhetorical style that will not only achieve a greater conceptual consensus, but also help make it both powerful and useful in line with other concepts in the practical and critical disciplines of rhetoric. To achieve the necessary scope in this conceptual development, the theoretical starting point of the book is a meeting between research traditions of style in rhetoric. One tradition has a particularly systematic character; mainly German, it provides a good overview of the state of affairs. Furthermore, most of these studies aim to place style within different areas of research – such as rhetoric, literary theory, aesthetics, or art history. Often, there is a short section on recent American rhetorical criticism, but this field is presented as a perspective rather than a central part of the account.

A number of recent style studies within the American tradition of rhetorical criticism, the other research tradition central to my project, are thus disregarded. In the twentieth and twenty-first centuries, American rhetorical criticism has developed into a strong tradition of rhetorical analysis of current and historical social discourses, theoretically grounded conceptual development, and criticism of the ethical and societal perspectives of specific statements and discourses. The style studies that are part of this tradition of rhetorical criticism are often highly original, and crucial in their contribution to the development of concepts of style within a modern and postmodern critical context. They produce insights into style as a concept in the discipline of rhetoric, just as they form the concept in a way that is useful for analyzing and understanding rhetorical discourse. At the same time, a theoretical connection to sociology, social science, linguistic research, and aesthetics helps to further open up the field. It is also characteristic that these studies take into account that rhetorical issues also arise outside the more traditional rhetorical areas and genres. Altogether, these studies have largely kept the concept of style crisp, and made it interesting to use in rhetorical theory and practice. However, a key feature of the American research tradition is the lack of a systematic account of the discipline's own research contribution in relation to other research in rhetorical style. Compared to the German scientific tradition, many major American style studies fail to take into account a convincing volume of other approaches to and definitions of style. The absence of a unifying effort to explain neighboring traditions within and outside American rhetorical criticism, and place its own contribution in relation to these traditions, results in a lack of discussions that could otherwise bring compelling theories and traditions into dialogue and increase our understanding of style.

My project strives to bring insights from different research traditions – including rhetorical, literary, and linguistic theories of metaphor – into dialogue with one another. The artefacts that are examined in the project are a blend of Danish rhetorical discourse and public debates of a more international nature. Danish rhetorical discourse, however, predominates. Although the Prime Minister's official address is included, smaller, more local political discourse is also made the object of study. This choice is founded in an interest in the vernacular and a conviction that this type of discourse is as important a practice as official discourse. Furthermore, the insistence on Danish rhetorical discourse contends that a smaller country is not necessarily less relevant. Many rhetorical concepts have been developed in critical analysis of cases that have *become* relevant to an audience of rhetorical critics because of the study. This, too, is my hope for this study; in fact, a basic sympathy – if not an immediate interest – would be the preferred attitude of the reader.

A Re-theorizing of Rhetoric and Style

The establishment of a broader theoretical platform in this project is intended to make rhetorical style sharper and more useful as an analytical and critical concept. It also sets an agenda for the discipline that will strengthen the theoretical side of rhetorical research. While the practical and application-oriented aim of rhetoric is both important and valid – and is strongly represented in, for instance, communication, teaching, and political debate – it does not cover the breadth of the discipline. Rhetoric has traditionally been driven by heavy knowledge interests in language, ethics, aesthetics, and social theory – and fortunately in many respects it still is today. This investigation seeks to strengthen research into rhetorical theory and thus also serves as a contribution to some of the ongoing disciplinary discussions in

Scandinavian and European research environments. Regarding these discussions, it is my stance that theoretical reflections should do more to set the defining framework for the practical application of rhetoric, rather than the reverse, as is often the case.

My concept of "rhetorical style" includes definitions of style in rhetorical theories past and present. It embraces traditional concepts of language, *elocutio*, and rhetorical figures, as well as more recent approaches to style as a performance of social identity. Rhetorical style may be *both* specific word choices or combination of words in a rhetorical message, *and* bodily gestures or aesthetic habits. Rhetorical style may be used intentionally and strategically to influence others, or it may be performed with no specific intention but to 'gather' socially, thus communicating social norms and motives rather than specific claims. In accordance with the broader rhetorical tradition, I understand rhetorical style as part of *rhetorica utens*, a practice that may be used to communicate, debate, argue, perform, and influence – and as a critical concept that may be employed analytically and critically to interpret and evaluate rhetorical practice. Rhetorical critics are most likely to recognize or develop rhetorical style on the basis of stylistic conventions, such as metaphor or stylistic tokens of ideology, or on the basis of patterns of signs and actions that work together as a unified system. In order to encompass the complexities of rhetorical style, I draw on two of its existing topoi – "style as dress" and "style as man" – and develop my own concept, "constitutive style."

The goal is to achieve a clearer understanding of some of the ways in which rhetorical style supplies the conceptual frameworks for reflecting, perceiving, arguing, and gaining influence in practical life. The study aims to advance both knowledge and practice in seeking to demarcate a very heterogeneous and sometimes also diffuse field. This is not a historical study that probes certain historical periods, or the development of the concept of style as such; rather, it is guided by an interest in producing knowledge through an examination of the validity of the concept of style through reasoning, discussion, analysis, and criticism.

Rhetorical analysis and criticism are well-established disciplines in American – and more recently European – rhetorical research, and it is important to emphasize that rhetorical analysis does not serve to illustrate a theoretical point, but rather is a substantial part of the study. Through rhetorical analysis one not only sharpens one's tools and explores their possibilities and range of uses; one also finds ways to adjust them or further develop the concept with a view to producing knowledge. Its outcomes will include greater insight into rhetorical discourse and a better understanding of the society of which it is a part. The analysis presents an evaluation of rhetorical discourse, which has a strong tradition in rhetorical research. Rather than making a critical judgment in regard to pre-established standards such as ideological and moral critique, I seek to evaluate the appropriateness of rhetorical criticism as concretely and contextually as possible. My project also examines and revises the norms by which artifacts, actions, and discourses are judged. These meta-critical statements should of course be seen in the light of a general influence on rhetoric by a host of late modern theories: an influence that has led to both the criticism of universal categories and the deconstruction of the value hierarchies on which they are based.

Following these initial observations, I will attempt to translate my promises of theoretical advancement and analytical significance into practice. The reading of the rhetorical style of the Irish rock singer Bono brings attention to the fact that rhetorical style, whether it is a strategic use of rhetorical figures or style in the sense of clothes, manners, and attitude, is intermingled with substantive political argument. The introduction concludes with a presentation of the structure and contents of each chapter.

Styling Rhetorical Strategy

"There are probably more annoying things than being hectored about African development by a wealthy Irish rock star in a cowboy hat, but I can't think of one at the moment," the American author Paul

Theroux states in an article titled "The Rock Star's Burden."[1] Few people with the slightest knowledge of popular culture would miss Theroux's allusion to Bono, the leading singer in the Irish rock band U2 (though one might also think of Bob Geldorf). Among his many achievements, such as organizing and participating in benefit concerts, Bono has met with influential politicians and world leaders in order to address the need to bring attention to Africa's problems.[2]

For a rhetorician, Bono makes an intriguing analytical artefact. While his speeches can be categorized easily enough as deliberative in an Aristotelian sense, his mandate to speak on the particular topic of African development is somewhat less obvious. Theroux lumps Bono together with other celebrities such as Brad Pitt, Angelina Jolie, and Bill Gates, and describes them as mythomaniacs addressing Africa's problems as if they were simply a question of sending more money. Thus, the title of his article alludes not so much to Rudyard Kipling's poem "The White Man's Burden" (1899) as to cultural imperialism, sneering at Bono and other celebrities for their philanthropic view that the rich have a moral obligation to help the poor. Conversely, Theroux, who constitutes his ethos as a former Peace Corps teacher in Malawi, articulates the problem as a matter of bad governance and the flight of well-educated Africans.

From a rhetorical perspective, the discussion of alternative interpretations is crucial to an understanding of the exigence and, finally, the status of the rhetorical situation – a key, but also much disputed, concept in rhetorical criticism. Equally complex is the question of the rhetorical audience. It must be constructed differently by Bono and Theroux. Where Bono and the other celebrities who do charity work constitute an audience of sympathetic and benevolent benefactors, Theroux's own discourse aims to engage participants with critical interpretive repertoires.

---

1 Paul Theroux, "The Rock Star's Burden," *The New York Times*, December 15, 2005.

2 Casper Fruergaard Schrøder, "Mit navn er Bono, og jeg er rockstjerne," *Retorikmagasinet* 60 (2006): 32.

A proper rhetorical analysis should not, however, rely on the words of the fiercest critic, but ought to consider Bono's own speeches first hand. While Theroux takes a cowboy hat to be an emblem of the glaring misfit between substance and style in Bono's activism, there is certainly more to say about rhetoric and style in relation to Bono's speeches. In a speech delivered at the Labour Party Conference in UK 2004, for instance, Bono claims that the Western world needs to understand, and hence conceptualize, the problems of Africa differently. Rather than arguing on the premises of charity, Bono argues from universal topoi of justice and human equality:

> there's no way we can look at Africa – a continent bursting into flames – and if we're honest conclude that it would ever be allowed to happen anywhere else. [...] You see, deep down, if we really accepted that Africans were equal to us, we would all do more to put the fire out. We've got watering cans; when what we really need are the fire brigades.[3]

That style should play a part in Bono's political life is not exactly astounding, considering his poetical and spirited authorship of U2's lyrics and his status as a performing artist. But the way he deploys the resources of style and rhetorical figures, the specific strategy and its specific purpose, deserves closer scrutiny. The fire metaphor announces a major crisis out of control, and the watering cans expose our means to control it as inadequate. But the defining change of topic is caused by another figure, the antithesis. Bono explicitly distinguishes "the soft argument for action" from "the more muscular one" by presenting them antithetically: "this is not about charity, it's about justice."[4]

Bono does not ignore the fact that his agency to speak about poverty cannot be taken for granted. As in many other speeches, he opens

---

3 Bono, Speech at the Labour Party Conference, September 9, 2004, http://www.atu2.com/news/transcript-of-bonos-speech-at-labour-party-conference.html.

4 Ibid.

this one with an allusion to the standard greeting at Alcoholics Anonymous meetings: "My name is Bono and I'm a rock star."[5] In Bono's case, the standing topos of public confession serves as recognition of whatever doubts the audience may have in regard to his ethos as a speaker on African poverty. As he goes on, he continues to undercut his speaking position as a serious political agent: "I heard the word party – obviously got the wrong idea."[6] The play on the word "party" through the rhetorical figure of *antanaclasis* (use of a word in two different senses) functions, of course, as a pun. It is meant to make the conference delegates laugh, and once more, the joke is on the (allegedly) misplaced speaker. But the rhetorical figure also structures the argument that there is a vital difference between rock music and politics.

Bono forestalls the objection that he is not qualified to speak about Africa since he is not "an economist. An NGO. An African farmer" by resorting to basal honesty and common sense: "But actually, I can see through these goggles. I know progress when I see it. And I know forward momentum when I feel it."[7] Still, Bono aims not to persuade on practical politics; on the contrary, he emphasizes the difference between his job and the jobs of Tony Blair and Gordon Brown:

> Listen, I know what this looks like, rock star standing up here, shouting imperatives others have to fulfil. But that's what we do, rock stars. Rocks stars get to wave flags, shout at the barricades, and escape to the South of France. We're unaccountable. We behave accordingly. But not you. You can't. You can't do that. See, we're actually counting on you.[8]

5 Ibid.

6 Ibid.

7 Ibid.

8 Ibid.

The alliterations (repetition of consonants) on "unaccountable," "accordingly," "can't," and "counting" heighten the intensity of the argument, while the *polyptoton* (a repetition of words derived from the same root) installs a radical rupture between "unaccountable" rock stars and politicians that people are "counting on." With a little help from rhetorical figures and a rock 'n roll style, which pairs grandiose vision with a lack of practical suggestions, Bono hereby transfers the political responsibility to the Labour leaders.

Another example of Bono's rhetorical and critical intervention can be seen a few years later, in 2007, when he stated his disappointment with the G8 summit held in Heiligendamm, Germany with *hyperbole*, *antithesis*, and *polyptoton*:

> This summit outcomes document isn't readable in any language, it's called a communiqué but it seems to have been deliberately designed not to communicate the real facts. Do they think we can't read or count? We are looking for accountable language and accountable numbers: we didn't get them today.[9]

In this press release, Bono uses a hefty antithesis to dissociate himself and the organization DATA from the G8 summit. The repetition of words derived from the same root ("it is called a communiqué but it seems to have been deliberately designed not to communicate") mocks the gap between appearance and intent. Arguing with rhetorical figures, he dissociates the ostensible purpose from a supposed intended strategy of dissolving the audience with a confused discourse that the people concerned with the G8 meeting can neither oppose nor agree to. Towards the end of the brief message, Bono tries to re-constitute an audience, a "we": "But we are not lost; right now it's the G8 that are lost." With a chiasmus, the "we" is turned against the G8 leaders

9 Bono, "More leaders slipping up than stepping up for Africa at this year's G8," August 6, 2007.

as the G8 leaders are turned against each other: "We've had plenty of fights with them this week – but they've had more with each other."[10]

To return to Theroux's attempt to incriminate Bono's stylized appearance, it may be granted that as a speaker, Bono relies heavily on style. However, the implied opposition between style and substance can be swept away as Bono uses rhetorical figures and style to argue his case. In establishing his agency as a spokesperson in the fight against poverty, Bono bases his arguments not on an appeal to charity, but on universal topoi of identification, humanity, and justice. And in a performance of rock star style, he intricately confirms the worst prejudices against celebrities working for charitable causes as he forestalls the standard objections. As the above analysis reveals, sensitivity to stylistic argument may lead to insights more nuanced than the general point that style cannot be separated from substance. Critical investment in style often pays off in ample observations that evince the many facets in style as the source of good reasons and agency in public debate.

Content and Chapters

Part I of *An Argument on Rhetorical Style* is devoted to the conceptual development of rhetorical style, Part II to studies of particular examples of rhetorical styles. In the first chapter on "Constitutive Style," I approach the conceptual definition by comparing the terms and designations most commonly connected with rhetorical style. On the basis of historical and conceptual theories on the prevailing definitions of style, I outline and define my own investigation as a reinterpretation of rhetorical style in the framework of constitutive rhetoric.

In chapter two, on "The Function of Rhetorical Figures," the questions of rhetorical figures and metaphors are examined in the larger context of style. Compared to the conceptual inquiry in chapter one,

10 Ibid.

the study of rhetorical figures proves more straightforward, as there are certain theories that are definitive of this particular field of study. The theories of rhetorical figures are closely intertwined with the theoretical framework for style that I put forward in chapter one. I probe these findings in different examples of public deliberation, notably a debate case on the possible harmful perspectives on the language of sexual assault in hip hop lyrics.

In chapter three, "Style and the Postmodern," I address some issues that have circulated in aesthetic, literary, and rhetorical theories in their discussions of style and the postmodern. In particular, I pay attention to rhetorical theories that address style as a construction, or as a performance of individual and public identity. Meanwhile, I maintain a focus on the strategic aspects of style, which are explored on a practical level in a case study of official public speaking and governance, notably the Danish Prime Minister's Opening Address. I conclude Part I with a summative discussion of the theoretical developments of the first three chapters.

Part II consists of three chapters exploring the practices of particular styles. Chapter four, "Feminine Style in Danish Local Politics," investigates "the feminine style," which traditionally prescribes the social norms for how females should behave and speak in public. However, my prime case study of a panel debate, which was part of a campaign advocating increased female participation in contemporary Danish local politics, proves to be a significant challenge for the theories of the feminine style.

In chapter five, "Provocative Style," I develop my own concept of a particular style that can be employed analytically and critically in rhetorical criticism. The concept challenges certain norms of public communication and their entailment of a normative, idealized rhetoric. In removing universal norms from the line of sight, it brings attention to the functions and strategies employed in provocations and polemics. Thus, the study of provocative style necessitates the recognition of contextual interpretations, as norms are constantly negotiated by publics. The exploration of provocative style revolves around an elaborated case study of a global debate about the insult and provocation of Jews.

In chapter six, I explore speechwriting, or logography, in terms of rhetorical style. The conceptual categories of style developed in chapter one and throughout *An Argument on Rhetorical Style* are set up as a theoretical framework in this field of rhetorical practice, which has hitherto been undertheorized. In the Conclusion, I recapitulate points arrived at and tie up loose ends.

Some of the chapters are rewritten versions of articles that that have been previously published. Thus, versions of chapter two appeared in *Rhetorica Scandinavica* 45 (2008) and Jens E. Kjeldsen and Jan Grue (eds.), *Scandinavian Studies in Rhetoric. Rhetorica Scandinavica 1997-2000* (2011). An earlier version of chapter five appeared in *Rhetorical Citizenship and Public Deliberation*, edited by Christian Kock and Lisa S. Villadsen (2012). A version of chapter six was published in *Rhetorica Scandinavica* 65 (2013). In addition, the analysis of Gyrithe Lemche's speech in chapter four has been published online at www.danmarkshistorien.dk.

PART I

Rhetorical Style as a Critical Concept

CHAPTER ONE

CONSTITUTIVE STYLE

When Per Stig Møller became the Danish Minister of Culture in 2010, the cultural sector welcomed him warmly. Møller had long been a substantial figure in Danish politics, and he was known as a highly literate and cultured person, as well as the author of several books. Politically, his latest and most significant successes were achieved when he served as foreign minister in the liberal–conservative Anders Fogh Rasmussen government. But in this period, Denmark had also participated in a war in Iraq without a mandate from the UN, and as secretary of state, Møller was partly responsible for this. Additionally, while Møller seemed subsequently to have forgotten the arguments he had advanced for the invasion of Iraq, his claims of Iraq's possession of weapons of mass destruction were thoroughly documented by the tabloid newspaper *Ekstra Bladet*. This inconvenience did not, however, affect the cultural elite's enthusiasm over the new minister, who had good taste, spoke French, and wrote books. Neither was the enthusiasm founded in warranted expectations of political substance – such as actual propositions or suggested solutions to cultural politics. In fact, he had said nothing that former ministers of culture despised by the cultural elite could not have said. Yet what Møller said seemed of great importance. It was simply a matter of style.

This analysis of Per Stig Møller's style is distilled from an essay originally published in Danish under a title that translates as "A Matter of

Style."[1] Although – or because – the portrait seems a shade polemical, it provides a rather accurate analysis of style and of how we perceive it to be superficial, shallow, and contrary to political substance. The issues of how we understand style, how we use the word "style" in everyday language, and how we approach style academically are the focus of the present study. I shall return to the portrayal of Møller's style at the end of the chapter.

In daily use, not all references to style correspond to the understanding endorsed in the example above. To look for another view, we need go no further than the nearest magazine stand, where the glossy covers offer fulfillment of our true selves through a certain haircut or outfit. Yet the notion of a correspondence between style and self, imbedded in the idea that style can function as a key to a human being's personality or identity, belies an understanding of style as mere embellishment. Moreover, the confusion regarding the meaning of style cannot be isolated to the level of everyday language. Theoretical discussions of style are just as often complicated by contrary definitions, and they increasingly partake in cross-disciplinary struggles to address a topic which bears the same name but engages scholarly traditions with different interests and goals. Consequently, the systematic study of style has long been thwarted by diffusion and ill-definition.

The present exploration aims neither to solve these inter-disciplinary problems, nor to provide an exhaustive overview of all branches of style. My research topic is "rhetorical style," which may be characterized as a manner of using language and cultural codes in rhetorical practice; it is my premise that the theories I engage with actually address the same problem, in one way or another. However, since the disciplinary tradition of style in rhetoric still seems to be an umbrella term rather than a defined topic, my study commences with further itemization in order to structure and define a manageable research field.

---

1 Rune Lykkeberg, "Et spørgsmål om stil," *Information*, March 27-28, 2010, 4.

Defining Rhetorical Style

In his conclusion to the book *Style – The Problem and Its Solution* (1969), Bennison Gray compares style to ether: "an entity with no attributes of its own, whose existence has never been proven, which is assigned the properties of whatever system it happens to be applied to, and therefore has numerous contradictory properties, and which, finally, can be discarded."[2] Refraining from fully subscribing to Gray's point of view, the entry on "Stil" in *Historisches Wörterbuch der Rhetorik* (1992-2009), however, admits to the complexity of style. It is a concept with several disciplinary and epochal manifestations, and a broadness already apparent in its etymology:

> στῦλος, stýlos (Pfeiler, Säule); stilus (Schreibgriffel, Schreibart; stilus für 'Schreibart' bereits bei Plinius d. J.); Stilo, Styl, Stiehl, Stil (Schreibart, Einheit der Ausdrucksform eines Kunstwerkes, eines Menschen, einer Zeit). Die Verwendung des Stilbegriffs knüpft im ersten Drittel des 15. Jh. an die übertragene Bedeutung von lat. *stilus* = *modus scribendi et dicendi* an.[3]

Etymologically derived from the word "stylus," a writing instrument, style comes to denote a unity of expression and a manner of writing and speaking. Moreover, the complexity of style is reflected in two related entries in the German lexicon, on "Elocutio" and "Stillehre, Stilistik," respectively. The three entries overlap on some points, occasionally with explicit cross-references, but the attempt to define separate topics is clear enough. After briefly comparing the content of these three entries, I will trace some distinctive features of "style" on which I can, eventually, anchor my own investigation.

---

2 Bennison Gray, *Style – The Problem and Its Solution* (The Hague: Mouton, 1969), 109.

3 Bernhard Sowinski, "Stil (lat. stilus; engl., frz. style; ital.stile)," in *Historisches Wörterbuch der Rhetorik*, vol. 8, ed. Gert Ueding (Darmstadt: Wissenschaftliche Buchgesellschaft 2007), 1393.

The entry on "Elocutio" is centered on the third part of the inventive process in the traditional rhetorical system (*partes rhetoricae*) and its later interpretations. As noted by Joachim Knape, the author of the lengthy entry on *elocutio*, even the earliest theorists of rhetoric were interested in language structure, and even *Rhetoric to Alexander* – the first Greek treatise on rhetoric, written by Anaximenes – was concerned with *lexis*. But it was not until the third book of Aristotle's *Rhetoric* that *lexis* and *phrasis* were examined systematically. In continuation of this work, Aristotle's pupil Theophrast wrote a monograph about *lexis*, which is mainly lost, but has been reconstructed. Both its rules for language usage and its taxonomy of figures together serve as a model for the chapters on *elocutio* in later treatises about rhetoric. The main categories of this systematic theory of *elocutio* are qualities of style (*latinitas*, *perspicuitas*, *aptum*, and *ornatus*) and genres of style (plain, middle, high). The category of linguistic choices, *ornatus*, has further subdivisions, of which the most significant are the rhetorical figures and the tropes. Later interpretations develop the system as a whole or in parts. In the twentieth century, elements that had traditionally been grouped as elocutionary – for instance, rhetorical figures or typologies of style – were revived as key issues in formalistic theories of literature, linguistics, and semiotics.[4]

The *Historisches Wörterbuch der Rhetorik* entry on stylistics, "Stillehre, Stilistik," covers the teaching of proper, expedient, and effective verbal expression, as well as the artful formation of an oral or written speech.[5] Originally, it referred to *elocutio*, the third of the five tasks of the speaker (*officia oratoris*), but beginning in the nineteenth

4 Joachim Knape, "Elocutio (griech. λέξις, léxis, φράσις, phrásis; dt. rednerischer Ausdruck, Stil; engl. diction, locution, elocution; frz. Elocution; ital. elocuzione)," in *Historisches Wörterbuch der Rhetorik*, vol. 2, ed. G. Ueding (Darmstadt: Wissenschaftliche Buchgesellschaft, 1994).

5 H. Mayer, "Stillehre, Stilistik (lat. bene dicendi praecepta, elocutionis ratio; eng. Stylistics; frz. Stylistique; its. Stilica)," in *Historisches Wörterbuch der Rhetorik*, vol. 9, ed. G. Ueding (Darmstadt: Wissenschaftliche Buchgesellschaft, 2007), 1.

century it became an autonomous discipline of prescriptive stylistics with a practical aim. A second meaning of "stylistics" applies it to a descriptive and analytic discipline involved in defining style as a theoretical concept, and in developing methods to analyze style; this branch is covered, we are informed, under the "Stil" entry, where it can be found under the description of academic research on style in the nineteenth and twentieth centuries.

Comparatively, the entry on "Stil" has a broader scope and is less centered on traditional rhetoric than the other two articles. As this topic comes closest to my own interest, my study of this entry will be a little more elaborate. Style – at least in its modern definition – is a key term in different disciplines, and thus it can be used to analyze or describe a wide range of objects. Yet some features remain the same, and it is because of these persistent, recognizable chunks that the comparison to ether, quoted above, falls flat. It is possible, after all, to speak generally of the modern meaning of style:

> Mit dem Begriff des <S.> und seinen lexikalischen Ausprägungen werden heute in den meisten Kultursprachen folgende Grundbedeutungen verknüpft: 1. die nach Stoff, Thema, Textsorte, Intention, Situation, Tradition und Individualität verschiedene Art der Ausprägung von Texten, Musikstücken und graphischen, bildhaften, architektonischen und plastischen Werken, oft künstlerischen Charakters; 2. Die Kennzeichnung auffallender wiederholter Verhaltensweisen im Leben und Tun eines Menschen (z.B. Lebensstil, Trainingsstil, Laufstil usw.); 3. ein positives Werturteil über Menschen und Gegenstände (z.B. Er/Es hat Stil!).[6]

According to Bernhard Sowinski, the author of the article on "Stil," three possible meanings lie at the heart of most modern understand-

6 Sowinski, "Stil," 1394.

ings of style: 1) The different and often aesthetic ways that texts or works of art may be shaped by content, genre, intention, situation, tradition, and individuality; 2) Repeated, conspicuous behavior in a person's life or actions;[7] or 3) A positive evaluation of people or artifacts.

In documenting the early history of style, Sowinski refers to both practitioners of rhetoric and style (such as Empedokles and Gorgias) and theorists. Here, in contrast to the encyclopedia articles on "Elocutio" and "Stillehre, Stilistik," Theophrast is passed by with the remark that his work is lost; instead, the description of style in ancient Greece focuses on the principles of language usage in the third book of Aristotle's *Rhetoric*. Later, the general Greek influence on Roman culture led to Greek rhetoric being adopted by the Romans. Practical and theoretical aspects of rhetoric were exercised in controversies over style ideals between supporters of a lofty Asian style and those who favored the *brevitas* of the Attic style. Several treatises on rhetoric were written in continuation of the concept of rhetoric and style passed down by the Greeks. In contrast to the elaborate taxonomies of *Rhetorica ad Herennium* (86-88 B.C.) and to Cicero's view that the beautiful should be reflected in the useful, style was at the center of *On the Sublime* by Longinus, who told the poets to strive for an elevated language in order to let divine light shine through the human soul. The sublime was achieved partly by a natural disposition and an ability to concentrate and to use pathos, but some aspects could also be learned, such as the construction of sentences and use of rhetorical figures. Closer to Cicero was Quintilian, who, in the twelve books of his *Instituio*

7 In his book *Stilistik*, Sowinski gives an elaborated account of this feature: "Alle Wörter, die das Wort 'Stil' als Grundbegriff enthalten (also z.B. Übungsstil, Kampfstil, Literaturstil, Epochenstil, Sprachstil, Lebensstil, Szenenstil, Baustil, Jugendstil usw.) haben gemeinsam, dass sie etwas kennzeichnen oder charakterisieren, meistens den im vorangehenden Wortteil gemeinten Bereich, z.B. die Literatur in 'Literaturstil', die Dramen in 'Dramenstil' usw., oder das dort genannte Tun, z.B. Kampf in 'Kampfstil', Training in 'Trainingsstil' usw." Bernhard Sowinski, *Stilistik. Stiltheorien und Stilanalysen* (2nd ed.) (Stuttgart: Metzler, 1999), 3.

Oratoria, addressed problems of style, also discussing it in terms of concepts other than *elocutio* (such as *genus orationis*, *genus Rhodium*, *Atticorum*, *dicendi genera*, and *modus orationis*). The teaching of *elocutio* is covered by book eight, in which the author demands that words be used with precision, clarity, beauty, and propriety. One of the theorists of style of the late Roman era mentioned by Sowinski is Hermogenes, a Greek rhetorician who replaced the hitherto established theory of three genres of style with a variety of shades (*ideai*).

From the Middle Ages up until the eighteenth century, most Latin grammars contained a draft of Latin rhetoric which remains fairly consistent: an overview of the speaker's tasks (*inventio*, *dispositio*, *elocutio*, *memoria*, *actio*), the three genres of rhetoric, the three levels of style, principles of words and syntax, errors of style, and a taxonomy of figures and tropes. In the description of *elocutio*, the word "stilus" is used increasingly, but it is not until the Renaissance that the word "style" obtains its modern meaning.[8]

In the modern history of "Stil," style was adopted by the aesthetic disciplines. In the middle of the eighteenth century, the German art historian J.J. Winkelmann applied the concept of style – which until this time had almost solely referred to language – to visual arts, architecture, and sculpture. His comparisons of style in ancient and contemporary artworks formed the basis of a kind of history writing centered on style in the arts. In art history, H. Wöllflin's comparative study of stylistic characteristics in the Renaissance and Baroque established a method of analyzing epochal characteristics of style. In the following years, this method of stylistic analysis was assimilated and developed further in art history and literary studies. Ironically, the increasing interest in style in literary and other aesthetic studies happened simultaneously with rhetoric's general demise and discredit. As style was loosened from the schematics of systematic rhetoric in the

---

8 Ibid., 1401 and 1406. See also Wolfgang G. Müller, *Topik des Stilbegriffs. Zur Geschichte des Stilverständnisses von der Antike bis zur Gegenwart* (Darmstadt: Wissenschaftliche Buchgesellschaft, 1981), 6.

nineteenth and twentieth centuries, studies of formal and functional elements proliferated into different modern, academic disciplines, such as structuralism, linguistics, communication, and speech-act theory.

To summarize the above outline of the three entries, "style" is characterized as distinct from the modern academic enterprise of linguistic analysis ("stilistik"), yet according to the logic of the circular references, in this sense the term "stilistik" is also an aspect of style.[9] Similarly, "style" is characterized as distinct from the practice and pedagogy of oral and written composition ("stillehre"), as well as from "elocutio," the systematically ordered third step of the *officia oratoris*. Yet the branches are also thoroughly enmeshed, with themes, traditions, and specific works reappearing throughout the three entries. Although the encyclopedia provides an overview of the contours of style, definite distinctions between style, stylistics, and *elocutio* are not the outcome. Rather, the lesson seems to be that the enterprises can only be provisionally defined since they are closely intertwined, and sometimes even identical.

This, however, does not hinder a search for a more qualitative, or substantial, definition of style. Some questions remain to be answered satisfactorily; for instance, how a term such as *style* maintains its at-

---

9 According to Rainer Rosenberg, style is also a disputed concept within a linguistic paradigm. It is defined differently depending on the scholarly traditions; however, a fundamental perception of style as a phenomenon of language persists: "Übereinstimmung besteht nur darin [...], daβ Stil als ein prinzipiell sprachliches Phänomen gefaβt wird. Als solches umfaβt es alle sprachlichen Ebenen von der Laut- und Klanggestalt über die Lexik und die Morphologie bis zur grammatikalisch-syntaktischen und zur Textebene, geht aber nicht über sie hinaus." Rainer Rosenberg, "Literarischer Stil," in *Ästhetische Grundbegriffe*, vol. 5, ed. K. Barck et al. (Stuttgart: Metzler, 2003), 658-659. For a systematic account of this understanding of stylistics, see Sowinski, *Stilistik.* A similar focus on linguistic aspects predominates in Ulla Fix, Andreas Gardt & Joachim Knape, eds., *Rhetorik und Stilistik: ein internationals Handbuch historicher und systematischer Forschung/ Rhetoric and Stylistics: an international handbook of historical and systematic research*, vols 1-2 (Berlin: Gruyter, 2008-2009).

traction and currency despite its obvious flaws and diffuse character. What is *style* thought to describe? Which specific quality do we believe is captured by the concept of style? And how do we account for at least the more significant differences in usage and application, along with the contradictory definitions?

These are some of the prime concerns of my investigation. Fortunately, serious groundwork has already been laid on the topic, notably by the German scholar Wolfgang G. Müller. As his thoughts serve as the principal foundation of my own theoretical framework of style, I shall account for his argument in some detail. I will then proceed with a discussion which can be outlined as follows: Since Müller's framework does not suffice to account for rhetorical studies of style shaped by postmodernist thought, we must seek a theoretical explanation in the rhetorical theories that do, particularly theories of constitutive rhetoric. An inquiry about what the revised understanding of style must mean for an understanding of *rhetoric* is embedded in these explorations, which will take us as far back as the Sophists. Concurrently, I return to the case of the Danish Minister of Culture in order to explore, analytically and critically, where this new theoretical perspective on style leads us. Finally, the chapter concludes with a formulation of the thesis that is examined in the study.

Style as Dress

In *Topik des Stilbegriffs. Zur Geschichte des Stilverständnisses von der Antike bis zur Gegenwart* (1981), Wolfgang G. Müller traces how two competitive and mutually exclusive topoi have governed the perception of style from antiquity until the twentieth century. The first is the Neoclassical topos of style as the dress of thought; the other is the fundamentally Romantic notion of an identity between style and the character of human beings. As for the organizing rhetorical concept, topos, Müller explains that his approach encompasses the traditional double nature of the topos, as it refers to the central argument and thought as well as to a commonplace – that is, a more proverbial understanding. It follows, as Müller points out, that the significance and impact of a topos is dependent on how remarkably it is articulated. This emphasis on actual wording is noteworthy in that Müller does not limit his own investigation to the actual usage of the word "style," but coherently traces the predominant topoi of style where "speech," "rhetoric," "art," "literature," or, simply, "language" is discussed.

One of the topoi that has dominated thinking on style is "style as the dress of thought" ("Der Stil als Einkleidung des Gedankens"), which incorporates the idea that style is an ornament or a garb in which the thought is dressed. It is a visual metaphor which, Müller notes, has its roots in antiquity, but since the primary focus of his book *Topik des Stilbegriffs* is on English seventeenth-century discussions of style, the Classical rhetorical perspective is not elaborated. In a later article, however, Müller implies that the topos coheres with the traditional concept of *elocutio*.[10] If we follow this thought, the topos of style as dress is founded in the idea of an inventive process in five steps which leads to a separation of rhetoric into five parts. According to the process metaphor of *officia oratoria*, the third task of the speaker – language and style – must be added to the already conceived argument, as the dress of thought.[11]

In *Topik des Stilbegriffs*, Müller states that in medieval times, when *elocutio* was at the center of rhetorical and poetic theories of style, the dress metaphor played an important role. Style is considered to have an aestheticizing function as embellishment, but also to respond to norms of propriety and *decorum* – which continues to have an influ-

---

10 In the article on "Style," in *Encyclopedia of Rhetoric*, Müller refers to "the traditional elocutionary concept of style as dress of thought," and grounds the topos of style as dress in *elocutio* rather than in neoclassicism: "a moderate restoration of the elocutionary idea of style occurred in the age of neoclassicism in the first half of the eighteenth century." Wolfgang G. Müller, "Style", in *Encyclopedia of Rhetoric*, ed. Thomas O. Sloane (Oxford: Oxford University Press, 2001), 751-752.

11 See also Marie Lund, "Retorisk stil," in *Retorikkens aktualitet. En grundbog i retorisk kritik*, ed. Marie Lund & Hanne Roer (Copenhagen: Hans Reitzel, 2014), 165-190.

ence on rhetoric far into the Renaissance: "Eine Rede ohne Zierrat wird als ebenso anstößig empfunden wie ein Mensch, der sich in der Öffentlichkeit nackt präsentiert. Dieser Aspekt der Schicklichkeit, des gesellschaftlichen Dekorums, ist, wie wir sehen werden, in vielen Stiltheorien, in denen die Kleider- und Schmucktopik weiterwirkt, von großer Bedeutung."[12]

From the late sixteenth century to the beginning of the eighteenth century, new ideals of style appeared; disputes over anti-Ciceronianism, science, and Puritanism all influenced the conception of style. Puritanism is characterized by an ideal of plainness, but not one that necessarily leads to a dismissal of rhetoric. In fact, the simplicity of language can be expressed in a dress metaphor, as even the God-given truth must be dressed fittingly. But to confuse matters, the same metaphor may also serve a different purpose – and idolize an ideal of nakedness according to which the truth must appear un-dressed, since dress is a sign of sin. Similarly, the scientific discourses associated with the Royal Society strive for a 'naked' style resembling mathematical plainness. Taken as a whole, the seventeenth century displayed a constant opposition between the two ideals: that the truth must be preached naked and that the truth must be dressed in its proper ornaments.

In the last quarter of the seventeenth century, a mild reaction against the plainness ideal tipped the scales in favor of a moderate support of rhetoric. As a representative of this tendency, Müller mentions Robert Ferguson, who devalued nakedness for the benefit of the persuasive force and argumentative value of rhetorical figures and rhetorical adornment. The dress metaphor returns as an argument for propriety and decorum in Ferguson's exhortations that a worthy subject matter should not be dressed in "gaudy Dress."[13]

---

12 Müller, *Topik des Stilbegriffs*, 53.

13 Ibid., 71. Robert Ferguson, *The Interest of Reason in Religion, with the Import & Use of Scripture-Metaphors; and The Nature of the Union Betwixt Christ & Believers* (London, 1675), 357-358.

To sum up Müller's exploration of the topos of style as dress, the dress metaphor is frequently decisive in Neoclassical theories of style, in which it is associated with social rank and decorum – both important aspects of style in the period: "Dieser in der Poetik des Klassizismus häufig betonte Nexus von Gesellschaftsklasse und sprachlicher Ausdrucksweise läßt den Stil vorzüglich als ein soziales Phänomen erscheinen."[14] Nevertheless, the topos originates from theory prior to the Neoclassical period, as it is, arguably, founded in the theory of *officia oratoria* and the concept of *elocutio*.

Style as Man

Even more profoundly than style as dress, the topos identifying style with the speaker's soul or personality has shaped thinking on style from antiquity to modern times. The congruence between speech and person is an essential component of a highly moral understanding of rhetoric among both Greeks and Romans. Notably, Isocrates found that mastering the art of speaking was a sign of virtuous thinking; it followed as a central argument that by perfecting his speech, man is able to perfect his moral character. The notion of interdependence between the speaker's moral character and his way of speaking persists in the Roman period, as evidenced by the stress placed by both Cicero and Quintilian on the ethical dimension of rhetoric. The theory of rhetoric as a moral discipline is developed in terms of the *vir bonus* ideal: Only a good man can be a perfect speaker. In the Renaissance and Baroque, the topos identifying character with style reappears, and once again it is part of a conspicuous moral agenda. The idea that the human being and his or her speech are interrelated is central to the humanist ideal of eloquence.

The first comprehensive English theory of style is identified by Müller as George Puttenham's chapter "Of Style," in the third book of his

14 Müller, *Topik des Stilbegriffs*, 79.

The Arte of English Poesie (1589). Exemplary of its time, it is centered on the topos of self-identification through style: "Stile is a constant & continuall phrase or tenour of speacking and writing, extending to the whole tale or processe of the poeme or historie, and not properly to any peece or member of a tale: but is of words speeches and sentences together, a certain contriued forme and qualitie, many times naturall to the writer, many times his peculiar by election and arte."[15]

In the sixteenth and seventeenth centuries, the topos of personal identification through style becomes the center of a debate about the imitation of Cicero. Erasmus of Rotterdam opposed the blind imitation of Classical authors and favored a style reflecting the personality. Still more anti-Ciceronian is Montaigne, who adds new significance to the topos of self-identification through style. Montaigne's goal is to find a language to express the individual personality of the author. He seeks a free individual self, the ultimate judge of opinion, and therefore his theory of style, which allows for the greatest possible naturalness, is distinct from the Renaissance unity of an "I." Rather, it is a Baroque, radical subjectivism, sometimes referred to as 'libertine,' whereby the individual presence stands forth with all his failures and weaknesses.[16]

In the later history of the topos of self-identification through style, one of the more important events is Comte de Buffon's dictum "Le style est l'homme même" in his *Discours sur le style*, delivered at the Académie Française on August 25, 1753. To Müller, this wording gives the topos its modern validity and confirms his thesis that the survival of a topos depends not only on the thought, but also on

15 Ibid., 26. Gladys Doidge Willcock & Alice Walker, eds., *The Arte of English Poesie* (Cambridge, 1936), 148. Puttenham's observations about the constant quality of style come remarkably close to the descriptions of modern style in *Historisches Wörterbuch der Rhetorik*, cited above. Likewise, as noted by Müller, Puttenham's view that individual style is either unconscious or a result of choice is still valid today.

16 Müller, *Topik des Stilbegriffs*, 35.

its particular expression in language. Indeed, it is due to Buffon's superb formulation that the old topos was revived with a freshness of thought, although the aphorism, when interpreted as an authentic expression of the author's personality in the spirit of the nineteenth century – as is most often the case – is taken out of its historical context. Rather, it should be perceived in the framework of the Enlightenment, where the understanding of "l'homme" has a stronger connotation of social character than it does in Romanticism: "In der Antike bezog sich der Topos in erster Linie auf das Ideal des vir bonus, der Wohlredenheit und Ethos, Rednergabe und vorbildliche Moral miteinander verband. Buffon meint in seiner Fassung des Topos mit 'l'homme' den 'grand écrivain' des Klassizismus mit seiner umfassenden Bildung, seinem rationalistischen Weltbild und seiner kultivierten Lebensart."[17] However, Müller does not dismiss as misplaced the vast number of Romantic interpretations of Buffon's dictum, taking them instead to be evidence of the formal vitality given the traditional topos by Buffon.

The direction taken by the theory of style in Romanticism and the following periods was towards an eradication of the "style is the dress of thought" topos and a propagation of contrasting topoi such as "style as the man," "style as the incarnation of thought," and "style as the nation." The final Romantic verdict over the Neoclassical dissociation of style and thought – and the related dress metaphor – was uttered by William Wordsworth: "If words be not (recurring to a metaphor before used) an incarnation of the thought but only a clothing for it, then surely will they prove an ill gift."[18] To Wordsworth, what matters are expressions "which are not what the garb is to the body but what the body is to the soul, themselves a constituent part and power or function in the thought."[19]

---

17 Ibid., 41.

18 Ibid., 90. William Wordsworth, *The Prose Works of William Wordsworth II*, ed. W. J. B. Owen & Jane Worthington Smyser (Oxford, 1974), 84.

19 Ibid.

For the Romantics, the dress metaphor is interpreted negatively as grounded in an understanding of style as external and superficial, a purely rhetorical adornment. In early Romanticism, the idea of individual style gained territory, but Müller underlines that two topoi were joined: that style is the human being in its unique individuality and that style is the incarnation of thought.[20] Although hardly identical ideas, Müller's linking of the two is clearly based on the observation that, fundamentally, they share a conception of style as an interrelation of form and content which evinces their topical kinship.

In the middle and second half of the nineteenth century, style became a central term in literary studies and art theory, with its leading principle being the topical identification of style and man. In Germany, a school of modern stylistics, analyzing style as the symptomatic expression of the personality of the author, was founded by the literature scholars Karl Vossler and Leo Spitzer.[21] In twentieth-century literary aesthetics, style was often considered to be the essence of the work's literary quality, but in contrast to earlier periods, the modern understanding – notably in the work of poets like Eliot and Rilke – is characterized by the objectivity and impersonality of the artwork. Although the modern discussions are about art rather than style, Müller argues that they are grounded in nineteenth-century style theory and can be considered new interpretations of the "style est l'homme même" topos: "Es handelt sich dabei nicht einfach um den alten Gedanken, daβ der Redestil eines Menschen unmittelbarer Ausdruck seiner seelisch-geistigen Verfassung ist (*oratio mentis imago*), sondern um die Vorstellung, daβ sich eine Persönlichkeit nur im Ringen mit der Sprache, m.a.W. in einem Akt authentischer Formgebung in ihrer einmaligen Besonderheit offenbart."[22]

The topos has been pushed even further by the French author Maurice Merleau-Ponty, who inverts the traditional relationship between

20 Müller, *Topik des Stilbegriffs*, 97.

21 Ibid, 176.

22 Ibid., 168.

man and style. Instead of seeing language as a simple instrument, he understands it as identical with the writer and the creation of meaning: "La langage cessait donc d'être pour l'écrivain (s'il l'a jamais été) simple instrument ou moyen pour communiqué des intentions données par ailleurs. *A présent, il fait corps avec l'écrivain, il est lui-même.* La langage n'est plus le serviteur des signification, il est l'acte même de signifier."[23] Perhaps it follows from Müller's inclusion of this statement in the style as the man topos that he must judge such an understanding to be extreme: "Mit dem Gedanken der Neukonstitution des Ich durch die sprachkünstlerische Leistung hat das moderne Verständnis der topischen Gleichung von Mensch und Stil eine extreme Ausprägung erreicht."[24] At least, a constructivist conception of language, whereby the speaker's identity and the content are thought to be created by and exist in discourse, seems to push the style as man topos to its limits.

It follows from the overall organization of Müller's book that in some historical periods, one topos prevails over and has more pertinence than the other. Other historical periods are, however, defined by the co-existence of the two topoi. Yet it is Müller's definitive point that the perceptions of style – and indeed of rhetoric and language – which are founded on the two topoi together cannot cohere. The two topoi are competitive in their view on style and language; they are, in fact, mutually exclusive, as epitomized by Müller:

> Das Grundproblem, das sich aus dem Nebeneinander der beiden unterschiedlichen Stilauffassungen ergibt, has die Diskussion über den Stil bis ins 20. Jahrhundert beschäftigt. Es handlet sich um die Frage, ob der Stil *incarnatio* oder *exornatio* sei, ob er unlöslich mit dem ausgesprochenen Gedanken verbunden, d.h. mitbeteiligt an der Konstituering des Gedankens

23 Ibid., 169-170. Maurice Merleau-Ponty, *Signes* (Paris, 1960), 295-296.

24 Müller, *Topik des Stilbegriffs*, 171.

> sei, oder ob er nur die äußere Form sei, in die ein bereits gefundener oder vorliegender Gedanke gekleidet werde.[25]

The resulting epistemological question, a conflict between differing understandings of style and rhetoric, may be summarized as one of whether style is an incarnation of thought or merely an exterior form, something we add to fully developed thought. Without damaging Müller's argument, we may condense the conflict into a perception of style (or rhetoric or language) as part of the constitution of the thought (or argument or identity) versus the idea that style is only an added form.

A Constitutive View

Whereas in most cases I highly value Müller's ability to generalize specific and concrete observations, I have a reservation in relation to the constitutive aspect of the style as man topos. In my view, there is a difference between the idea that style and thought are one – or that we can infer the speaker's personality from his or her style – and the idea that thought, argument, and character are constituted rhetorically. It is a conflict which is blurred by Müller's use of the term "constitutive," which sometimes means that it is fundamental to or an inseparable part of the very content, but other times refers to the more wide-reaching idea – which Müller names a "Neukonstitution," in reference to Merleau-Ponty – that the identity of the speaker or the thought is constituted in language. In this particular case, the style as man topos is made to include what are, essentially, two different paradigms of thought; and in my view, this stretches the topos too far. Although I support Müller's identification of, for instance, the style as man and style as thought topoi because I concede that they are grounded in a mutual understanding of a

---

25 Ibid., 56.

relationship between form and content, I object to what in this case appears to be a confusing and unproductive amalgamation of two different epistemologies.

Instead, I propose that we add a topos that we may refer to as "style as constitutive," and that we distinguish it from the style as man topos. To take the discussion of "constitutive" beyond the ambiguities of casual usage, I will ground it in the discussions of the critical concept of "constitutive rhetoric" as it has been developed primarily by the Canadian rhetorical critic Maurice Charland in his article "Constitutive Rhetoric. The Case of the *Peuple Québécois.*"[26]

In the place of a transcendent audience, a collection of individuals who can be persuaded by discourse, Charland introduces an understanding of audience as a rhetorically constituted collective identity. Charland is indebted to Kenneth Burke's proposal of "identification" as the key term of the rhetorical process.[27] Contrary to theories centered on "persuasion," which imply the existence of an agent who is free to be persuaded, a rhetorical theory based on identification "does not posit a transcendent subject as audience member, who would exist prior to and apart from the speech to be judged, but considers audience members to participate in the very discourse by which they

---

26 Maurice Charland, "Constitutive Rhetoric: The Case of the *Peuple Québécois,*" *The Quarterley Journal of Speech* 73 (1987): 2.

27 The appointment of "identification" as an *alternative* to "persuasion," is, however, Charland's contribution. To Burke, "identification" is inextricably linked with "persuasion": "As for the relation between "identification" and "persuasion": we might well keep it in mind that a speaker persuades an audience by the use of stylistic identification; his act of persuasion may be for the purpose of causing the audience to identify itself with the speaker's interests; and the speaker draws on identification of interests to establish rapport between himself and his audience. So, there is no chance of our keeping apart the meanings of persuasion, identification ("consubstantiality") and communication (the nature of rhetoric as "addressed")." Kenneth Burke, *A Rhetoric of Motives* (Berkeley: University of California Press, 1965), 46.

would be 'persuaded'."[28] Thus, constitutive rhetoric opposes an Aristotelian notion of rhetoric as persuasion, which assumes that audiences are given and extra-rhetorical. Instead, constitutive rhetoric permits us to regard the very formation of subjects as a rhetorical process. Applied to Charland's analytic case study, the constitutive rhetoric of the movement for Quebec sovereignty, subjects are not persuaded to support sovereignty; instead, support for sovereignty is inherent to the subject position addressed by pro-sovereignty rhetoric.

Clearly, the theory of constitutive rhetoric has radical implications for the study of rhetoric, as it opposes rhetorical studies grounded in the tradition and reception of Aristotle's thoughts on rhetoric and audience up to the present day. As noted by Charland, constitutive rhetoric is a symbolically based critique of humanist ontology, a deconstruction of the transcendent subject, developed by structuralism and post-structuralism: "From such a perspective, we cannot accept the 'givenness' of "audience," "person," or "subject," but must consider their very textuality, their very constitution in rhetoric as a structured articulation of signs. We must, in other words, consider the textual nature of social being."[29]

Notwithstanding the potential of undermining traditional rhetoric, Charland does not turn his critique into a direct confrontation of opposing views. Instead, he allows for a combination of constitutive rhetoric and the traditional rhetorical notion of *persuasio*. Thus, according to Charland, constitutive rhetoric is logically prior to persuasion. Once presented in terms of the theory of constitutive rhetoric, a subject becomes the required audience for a rhetoric of persuasion.[30]

---

28 Charland, "Constitutive Rhetoric," 133.

29 Ibid., 137.

30 As Charland puts it, "to be interpellated is to become one of Black's personae and be a position in a discourse." Ibid., 138. Apart from this, Black's connection of stylistic tokens and discursive identity formation is a valuable technique for analyzing style. Black, Edwin, "The Second Persona," in *Contemporary Rhetorical Theory*, ed. John Louis Lucaites et al. (New York: The Guildford Press, 1999).

Yet this interpretation corresponds poorly with the underlying assumption that an identity position – which owes its existence to discourse and must be practised and rehearsed discursively to exist – can never be completely stable and consistent. Indeed, elsewhere Charland stresses that the interpellation of subjects – in Althusser's sense – is not restricted to one hailing, but is ongoing.[31]

In a later article, Charland introduces a distinction between constitutive rhetoric as a genre and as a theory.[32] As a genre, constitutive rhetoric is appropriate to certain rhetorical situations, so-called "founding moments," and applies primarily to rhetoric that asserts a collective identity for its audience. In terms of *de facto* rhetorical genres, it can be found in texts like constitutions and declarations, but also in the rhetoric of social movements and nationalist political campaigns. As a theory, however, constitutive rhetoric maintains its radical edge, and Charland stresses its distinction from Aristotle's persuasive rhetoric, which has dominated rhetorical theory:

> He considered rhetorical practice to be the art of crafting speech to persuade an audience that is called upon to render a judgment regarding a contingent question. Aristotle's Rhetoric is a guide to invention that stresses the need to offer proofs that exploit the typical presumptions, values, character, and affective dispositions of a given audience. In doing so, Aristotle does not consider the role of rhetoric in producing the very identity and character of an audience.[33]

In contrast, Charland traces the origin of the constitutive model to the Sophists, who knew the capacity of language to transform the very experience of being, and who "recognized discourse as produc-

---

31 Charland, "Constitutive Rheoric," 138.

32 Maurice Charland, "Constitutive rhetoric," in *Encylopedia of Rhetoric*, ed. Thomas O. Sloane (Oxford: Oxford University Press, 2001).

33 Ibid., 616.

tive of the very categories by which the world, and indeed the self, are understood."[34]

For my part, as I understand the meaning of "theory," it is general and generalizable, and in the case of constitutive rhetoric, the "theory" applies to a critical conceptualization of an understanding of rhetorical effect. It follows that as a theory – if theory is to achieve its meaning as a consistent structuring of thought – it cannot be combined with another theory, such as rhetoric perceived as persuasion. Similarly, the distinction between constitutive rhetoric as "genre" and "theory" is self-contradictory. If constitutive rhetoric possesses the 'universality' of a theory, it accounts for rhetoric in general and therefore applies to all rhetorical genres. Simply put, a theory of constitutive rhetoric does not need to be seconded by a category of constitutive genre.[35] Therefore, as much as I value Charland's critical theory of constitutive rhetoric, I object to the combination of constitutive rhetoric and persuasion, and to the distinction between theory and genre.

I will now turn to a discussion of the effects and perspectives of constitutive rhetoric in some later studies. While the radical implications for traditional rhetoric were somewhat downplayed by Charland, his theory has been a point of reference for both 'generically' and 'theoretically' inclined studies. Indeed, the distinction between 'theory' and 'genre' seems to have some currency in the description of the research traditions. Apparently, the critical interest has been strongest in the *genre* of constitutive rhetoric. As I am not convinced by the separation of theoretical and generic, or situational, aspects, I will in the following engage with some of the discussions related to "founding moments," although my own primary agenda relates to the more general aspect of constitutive rhetoric.

---

34 Ibid., 617.

35 However, a continuum of more or less assertive uses of constitutive features could be useful to account for the range and varieties of constitutive rhetoric.

Constitutive Rhetoric: Strategy and Effect

If persuasion is no longer operative as an explication of rhetorical effect, then how do we account for the successes or failures of rhetoric? Or rather, how do we – in constitutive terms – account for the fact that audiences are sometimes not 'persuaded'? To establish what the practical and strategic outcome of constitutive rhetoric may be, I will examine some second-generation studies of constitutive rhetoric. Two more recent studies develop the conceptual framework while reflecting on the consequences of a failed constitutive rhetoric and seeking to explain the theoretical circumstances for the failure.

In Charland's view, contradictory subject positions may exist simultaneously within a culture, and the success of a new constitutive rhetoric depends on the extent to which it offers new subject positions that resolve or contain experienced contradictions. However, as the American rhetorical critic Helen Tate asserts, Charland's study does not "take into account the complexities of the rhetorical culture in which they operate and how those discursive formations may play out over time." [36] Additionally, Tate observes that as his case identifies only one constitutive rhetorical artifact, he does not account for the complex of competing narratives. In Tate's explorative study of the ideological effects of a failed constitutive rhetoric, she detects a failure on behalf of white lesbian feminists to constitute all feminists as lesbians. Their constitutive rhetoric aimed at identifying feminism with the rejection of heterosexual oppression and heterosexuality as such, but it failed because most heterosexual feminists and lesbians of color rejected the narratives. This attempt to constitute an audience amounted to more than simply a rhetorical failure; Tate argues that the ideology of political lesbianism provided the rhetorical resources for antifeminism by creating a powerful counter-narrative to feminist identity.

---

36 Helen Tate, "The Ideological Effects of a Failed Constitutive Rhetoric: The Co-option of the Rhetoric of White Lesbian Feminism," *Women's Studies in Communication* 28, 1 (2005): 8.

The conceptual enhancement provided by Tate enables the critic to account for the complexities of competing narratives, and, in turn, to explain with greater accuracy the power and limitations of constitutive rhetoric in specific rhetorical circumstances. It also gives the conceptual basis for explaining how a failed constitutive rhetoric might result in strengthening the narratives of an opposing view. A similar lack of resonance with the material realities and previously articulated identities of an attempted constitutive rhetoric can be found in a study of the failure of the American President G. W. Bush's Iraq war rhetoric conducted by the American rhetorical critic Kenneth S. Zagacki. According to Zagacki, thePresident addressed the Iraqi people by employing "prophetic dualism," a rhetorical framework for interpreting American foreign policy that divides the world into the forces of good (the United States) and the forces of evil (America's enemies).[37] President Bush's rhetoric addressed Americans as givers of democracy and freedom, and the people of Iraq as the recipients, a constitution that could only last so long as democratization made progress. More specifically, he addressed an audience of Iraqis that he believed was already consubstantial – in Burke's sense of the term – with the very identity he sought to call into existence.[38]

However, Bush did not account for the fact that identities and narratives were already rhetorically constituted, in particular those of the Shiites and Sunnis; additionally, the Shiites and Sunnis were also provoked by the American occupation to enact their own ethnic and political identities.[39] Consequently, when Iraqis resisted President Bush's notion of an Iraqi democratic founding, he sought to define

---

37 Kenneth S. Zagacki, "Constitutive Rhetoric Reconsidered: Constitutive Paradoxes in G.W. Bush's Iraq War Speeches," *Western Journal of Communication* 71, 4 (2007): 273.

38 Ibid., 273-274.

39 Drawing on Judith Butler's theories of subjection and power, Zagacki suggests that for Iraqi insurgents, the imposition of American power provided "the very condition of 'existence and the trajectory of desire' as these were marshaled into

away the resistance within the confines of a prophetic dualist frame. As a better alternative, Zagacki suggests that political addresses should not only contain some signs of the audience's oppositional ethnic or religious positions, but also rearticulate existing subject positions to encourage a more reflexive democracy in Iraq.

Regarding my objection to Charland's combination of epistemological paradigms, Tate and Zagacki offer interpretations of constitutive rhetoric that do not resort to an inclusion of Aristotelian rhetoric. Furthermore, their critical leads are compelling, in my view, because they loosen constitutive rhetoric somewhat from the ideology-critical context to which it was tied by Charland.[40] Instead of viewing constitutive rhetoric solely through "a hermeneutics of suspicion" (Charland's words), these studies allow for a focus on the specific purpose and effect of rhetorical strategies within a constitutive rhetoric. When constitutive rhetoric is tied tightly to ideology criticism, the task of the critic is limited to disclosing how the constituted subject positions are inscribed within a power structure. Conversely, when it is regarded as a theory about rhetorical effect, it can be bracketed into rhetorical strategies that may, in turn, be viewed as *more* or *less* appropriate, expedient, and desirable within a specific rhetorical context. An additional quality of Tate and Zagacki's approach is that, as a consequence of a concern with the conditions for success and failure, constitutive rhetoric is also examined in terms of its productive and inventive potential – that is, how a theory of constitutive rhetoric can

---

the insurgency." Ibid., 288, and Judith Butler, *The Psychic Life of Power. Theories in Subjection* (Palo Alto: Stanford University Press, 1997).

40 In his article in the Oxford Encyclopedia, Charland identifies the theory of constitutive rhetoric as "critical rhetoric," which refers to ideological theory as developed by the Frankfurt School and French poststructuralism, "seeking to account for the discursive construction of power." As such, the theory of constitutive rhetoric is "fundamentally skeptical, because it refuses to take identity [...] as given. Rather, constitutive rhetoric calls attention to the historically contingent character of identity and its dependence upon discourse." Charland, "Constitutive Rhetoric" (2001), 618.

be used to construct a better alternative through a more considered strategy.

A Theory of Rhetorical Possibilities

Much the same effort to make constitutive rhetoric operational as a critical concept is to be found in the perhaps less apparent, yet even more influential, 'theoretical' heritage of constitutive rhetoric. Gerard A. Hauser, at least, claims that the concept of constitutive rhetoric has been the dominant theoretical school among rhetoricians in the United States since the late 1980s.[41] According to this view, rhetoric is strategic and instrumental and can be taught and practised as a method, but it is also a social practice which constructs a reality. As rhetorical action, it constitutes our very identities as meaningful subjects in relation to conditions in the world – as well as to the meaning of those conditions – and it frames a world of moral actions and consequences for its audiences. Similarly, it is a social practice that is constitutive of communication itself – for instance, the conditions for the activities of deliberation or negotiation. As such, rhetoric is constitutive of the social relations involved in this rhetorical action, notably the recognition of the value of opposing views.[42]

This late modern theory of rhetoric necessitates a re-reading of one of the core concepts of American rhetorical criticism: the rhetorical situation. In a rhetoric influenced by various aspects of postmodern theories, the rhetorical situation is perceived as structured according to a logic of articulation, rather than of influence. According to the rhetorical theorist Barbara Biesecker, a re-reading of the rhetorical situation which puts Jacques Derrida's concept *différance* into play

---

41 Gerard A. Hauser, *Introduction to Rhetorical Theory* (2nd ed.) (Prospect Heights: Waveland Press, 2002), 288.

42 Ibid., chapters 1-3.

makes the production of identities and social relations possible.[43] As a consequence, the exigence of the situation will not be considered given or objective as in Lloyd F. Bitzer's theory, but as a product of how we have been addressed and how we have interacted with the discourse.[44] As such, situations are dynamic and polysemous, reflecting changing contexts as well as our interpretations. Still, the constitutive view does not lead to relativism and to denial of the real world; as Hauser maintains, events actually occur, yet their significance in the ways they are perceived and resolved is socially constructed.

In my view, constitutive rhetoric is a theory of rhetoric, that is, a theoretical explanation of rhetorical language and its effects. As such, rhetorical language constructs a social practice *and* may be turned into particular rhetorical strategies. In both respects, the result may be deemed favorable – or not. It depends on the rhetorical discourse, the particulars of the rhetorical situation, and also, to some extent, the frame and focus of the critic. However, if the itinerary is fixed and the result is given in advance, a critical investigation becomes superfluous.

Instead of exposing of the lures of language, I suggest that we explore the more inventive side of constitutive rhetoric and style – a view of language that was already held by the Sophists: "The power of Gorgias's oratory is said to have been based in its capacity to enthrall an audience, not addressing their reasoning faculty, but poetically transforming their very experience of being."[45] Rejecting a transcendent truth and therefore arguing from probability, the Sophists were thought of as expounding a playful and experimental approach to language as "a creative force for shaping possibilities."[46]

---

43 Barbara Biesecker, "Rethinking the Rhetorical Situation from within the Thematic of Différance," in *Contemporary Rhetorical Theory*, ed. John Louis Lucaites et al. (New York: The Guildford Press, 1999).

44 Hauser, *Introduction*, 50.

45 Charland, "Constitutive Rhetoric" (2001), 616.

46 Hauser, *Introduction*, 29. This attitude prevails in Gorgias' "Encomium of Helen," in which the defense of Helen is based on an argument about the inherent power

Similarly, using the Sophists as a locus of the rhetorical, Susan Jarratt has characterized their common ground as "the primacy of human knowledge, possibilities for non-rational and emotional responses to the whole range of discourse types, a fundamental understanding of knowledge and values as historically contingent, a recognition of all discourse as 'rhetorical', an integral relationship between theory, practice and the political sphere."[47] Moreover, she links the revival of the Sophists in Classical rhetoric to a contemporary critical context in which knowing has become subject to analysis under the wider heading of discursive practice.[48] A similar path has been trodden by, among others, Robert L. Scott, who sought to establish a rhetorical epistemology originating in the Sophists. According to Scott, "Man must consider truth not as something fixed and final but as something to be created moment by moment and with which he must cope."[49] More recently, the rehabilitation of the Sophists has been based on the inventive potential of their rhetorical theory: "What Plato later termed *rhêtorikê* was not so much a knack for flattery as it was the novel production of a type of discourse capable of fusing logic with

---

of language and speech.

47 Susan Jarratt, *Rereading the Sophists. Classical Rhetoric Refigured* (Carbondale: Southern Illinois University Press, 1991), xviii–xix.

48 Ibid., xix. Jarratt's examples include Nietzsche's attempt to explode the 'scientific' basis of philosophy and natural law, Foucault's investigation of how disciplinary rules establish themselves, and Derrida's deconstruction of the binary structure of Western thought.

49 Robert L. Scott, "On Viewing Rhetoric as Epistemic," in *Professing the New Rhetorics. A Sourcebook*, ed. Therese Enos & Stuart C. Brown (Englewood Cliffs: Prentice Hall, 1994), 318. Note, however, Jarratt's objections to the term "epistemic": "For Aristotle, rhetoric is concerned only with practical knowledge [...] and is excluded from the realm of *episteme*, the certain knowledge which constitutes scientific understanding. Thus, for a movement against an Aristotelian rhetoric to call itself 'epistemic' in the loose sense of 'knowledge-generating' betrays an insensitivity to historical sources of the term." Jarrett, *Rereading the Sophists*, 123.

poetics to give form to the collective experience of citizenry in *kairotic* situations."[50]

To account for the third topos of 'style as constitutive,' I will, therefore, confine my investigation to the radical, 'sophistic,' and productive elements of the theory of constitutive rhetoric. While the discussion above is about rhetoric and constitutive rhetoric, it is obviously also – by means of the synecdoche – about rhetorical style. The scope of the present investigation is to narrow the focus and study more closely the aspects that are and have traditionally been associated with style, such as specific language use, rhetorical figures, and aesthetic, sensual, and cultural reference in rhetorical practices such as speeches and speechwriting, debates, and political campaigns. I will now return to our introductory example about the style of the Danish Minister of Culture in order to explore analytically how constitutive style operates and how it differs from the prevailing definitions.

A Criticism of Style

From this overview of style it becomes clear that Lykkeberg's article on the style of the Danish Minister of Culture is founded on what would be considered a topos of style as dress in Müller's theoretical framework. As such, this interpretation of style is congenial with the Neoclassical emphasis on social rank and propriety. To the cultural elite, the minister excelled in having the personal qualities of a cultured and highly educated person; he was a man of excellent taste and impeccable manners; in short, a man of the world. The contrast to the previous, conservative ministers of culture was not to be missed, in particular to Møller's immediate predecessor, Brian Mikkelsen. As one of Mikkelsen's many *faux pas*, he launched a political program of national 'culture canons' for the arts, but failed to pronounce the

50 Nathan Crick, "The Sophistical Attitude and the Invention of Rhetoric," *Quarterly Journal of Speech* 96, 1 (2010): 40.

word 'canon' correctly; he made the blunder of pronouncing the word in English rather than Danish. Surely, the cultural sector would not have to endure such humiliation with Per Stig Møller at the helm.

Rune Lykkeberg, the writer of the essay, portrays style as an exterior, surface phenomenon which precludes political substance, while still remaining loyal to Müller's description of the topos of style as dress. With great accuracy, Lykkeberg points out that Møller's personal style is utterly bereft of anything which has to do with actual political propositions or ideas. Graver still, his grand style is also opposed to a virtuous character, the article's central argument being the paradox of public excitement over a politician who has proven to be unreliable and untrustworthy.

More implicit is Müller's other topos, style as man. Behind the obvious scorn of a contemptuous writer, it is possible to distinguish another view on the new minister's style. From the perspective of the cultural elite, Møller's style is read as a sign of the skills and cultural competence of the man, and as such, his style is highly relevant to their political expectations. Unlike former ministers who were mostly keen on sports, Møller is actually likely to possess some sense of the art and culture for which he will have responsibility. In this respect, it was perhaps no wonder that the cultural sector showed signs of relief at having a minister who so obviously incarnated culture and *bildung*. From this perspective, it was also a matter of style, but it was a style grounded in the Romantic topoi of style as individual character and substance.[51]

---

51 The view was expressed in the ensuing debate on the newspaper's internet pages by a reader named Michail Larsen, who summed up a dilemma: "Would you rather have a custodian of neo-liberal/old-conservative 'culture' (with emphasis on commerce and tradition), or would you prefer a person who sometimes lies but at least has spirit?" *Information*, March 28, 2010 (my translation). The point of view was applauded by one of the newspaper's own reporters, Annegrethe Rasmussen, in another comment from March 29, 2010. See both entries on www.information.dk/228 398#comments.

Evidently, both of Müller's stylistic topoi apply. Additionally, I have introduced a third topos, the conception of style as constitutive of identity and political action, and in the following I will explore how it may be developed in relation to the same case study. One way of approaching the analysis could be to focus on an actual political initiative taken by the new Minister of Culture. Within the first few months, Per Stig Møller, on behalf of the Danish state, bought the vicarage of the pastor and poet Kaj Munk, who was executed by the Nazis during the German occupation. The press and political commentators immediately linked this political initiative to Per Stig Møller's own authorship, since he had written several books on Kaj Munk. Munk was an ambiguous figure, but he was primarily known to posterity as a person who fought the battle of the word against the Nazis in World War II – and paid with his life. In this way, Per Stig Møller's own fight for freedom of speech on the global political scene offered itself as a relevant context for an interpretation of this political action. Thus, the praise and political elevation of Kaj Munk's battle came to mirror Møller's battle for democracy and freedom of speech in Iraq, as well as in the Danish cartoon crisis provoked by satirical drawings of the Muslim prophet Muhammed.

But if this is style, what kind of style is it? I have contextualized my interpretation of Per Stig Møller's style within a pattern of relevant actions in order to detect a coherence of behavior which can be identified as a style. It is an interpretation based on judgments of probability and relevance, rather than on an essentialist view of the character of man. Neither is it based on an understanding of style as propriety, a social quality which is essentially unattached to the political matter or the personality. It is, in other words, a sense of style which cannot be identified with either the style as man or style as dress topoi. Instead, it is an understanding of style as constitutive and performative, resulting in an analysis of how Per Stig Møller performs or shapes his own political identity. As a Minister of Culture, his political decisions and actions are part of a re-articulation of his earlier merits and experiences, and joined together, they form a coherent style. In this sense, the understanding of style is inseparable from the understanding of political substance.

I have suggested this definition of style in addition to two well-established concepts of style, and as a third topos, it raises some questions about the status of these topoi and their interrelation. In Müller's history of style, the style as dress topos was eradicated with Romanticism and the predominance of the competing topos, style as man. If we follow this thought, style as dress, which is essentially the foundation for the perception of *elocutio*, should not have any pertinence in the modern meaning of style. However, this is far from an accurate depiction of our everyday usage of the word *style*, as is revealed by the analysis of the article on the Danish minister's style. Neither is it an accurate description of rhetorical theory, as I will argue in chapter two.

As I see it, all three conceptions of style play active parts in shaping our perception of style, and as for everyday use, I believe that all three perceptions of style are practised. Accordingly, the critical developments of the topoi of style are of great value because they have provided sharp analytical tools for engaging critically with an enhanced understanding of both the way we perform style and the way we perceive of it. However, although I regard all three topoi of style as useful critical concepts, I do not believe that they are equally pertinent. My own understanding of style is influenced by the theories governed by postmodern thought in which style is understood to be a constitutive quality, something to be performed.

In the following chapters, I will discuss some recent rhetorical theories of style, and it will be my thesis that the view they share cannot be grasped by the two traditional topoi of style offered by Wolfgang G. Müller. As predominantly postmodern rhetorical theories of style, they adhere to a different theoretical topos that does not converge with either ornamental or referential qualities; rather, they are constitutive of thought, argumentation, social relations, communicative action, identity, and gender. It is on this new, common ground that the present exploration seeks to establish an arena for reflecting on style in both contemporary rhetorical scholarship and rhetorical discourse.

CHAPTER TWO

THE FUNCTION OF RHETORICAL FIGURES

In the rhetorical tradition, a systematic and elaborated account of style and rhetorical figures is found in the theories of *elocutio*, the central category in the division of rhetoric into five *partes rhetorices*. According to this Classical tradition, developed by Theophrast and taken over by Cicero and Quintilian, there are four virtues of style: *puritas*, *perspicuitas*, *aptum*, and *ornatus*. Besides the qualities of clarity and correctness of language, the speech must be appropriate to the subject, as well as to the speaker, the audience, and the rhetorical situation. Fourth, and finally, it is demanded that rhetorical language be well equipped. At least, the Norwegian rhetoric historian Øivind Andersen argues that the idea of production and equipment captures the meaning of *ornatus* (Latin) and *kataskeve* (Greek) better than the straightforward translation of ornament, embellishment, and fancy dress.[1] Similarly, the British historian of rhetoric Brian Vickers has underlined the strength associated with *ornatus*:

> This word is inevitably rendered in English as 'ornament', with the unfortunate connotation of 'adornment', the use of unnecessary trappings or incidental decoration. But as George Kennedy pointed out, 'to the Roman ear the word "ornament"

1 Øivind Andersen, *I retorikkens hage* (Oslo: Universitetsforlaget, 1995), 65.

suggests distinction and excellence, the possession of resources ready for any challenge: it is a vital and useful quality,' which 'aids the orator's practical purpose, for by it he compels attention and bends the audience to his will'. Walter Ong noted independently that in Latin *ornamentum* signified 'equipment or accoutrements,' a soldier's 'gear' or weapons, and has nothing to do with purely ornamental devices.[2]

In the elocutionary taxonomy, *ornatus* has three subdivisions: choice of words, combination of words, and thirdly – the main focus of this chapter – rhetorical figures. As Andersen notes, the term *figures* serves both as a general heading of the whole field and as a more specialized subcategory, distinctive from tropes.[3] As a rule of thumb, the term *trope* designates the 'figurative' use of single words, where *figure* relates to more words or sentences. Analogous to the teaching of *ornatus* and rhetorical figures is the theory of three levels or types of style – the simple, the middle, and the elevated – which was also developed by Theophrast. The type of style was determined by three factors: choice of words, use of rhetorical figures, and syntax.

This brief summary of the traditional teachings of *elocutio* serves as a platform for the discussion in the present chapter. Whereas the first chapter was devoted to a conceptual development of style, based on the foundation of two stylistic topoi provided by W. G. Müller, the second takes stock of contemporary research on rhetorical figures. The general aim of this chapter is to position the 'latest findings' on rhetorical figures in the general theory and argument of style. In establishing this dialogue, I hope to increase the understanding of how style and rhetorical figures relate to each other. Furthermore, I intend

---

2 Brian Vickers, *In Defence of Rhetoric* (Oxford: Clarendon, 1988), 314; George A. Kennedy, *Quintilian* (New York: Twayne Publishers, 1969), 81; Walter Ong, *Ramus. Method and the Decay of Dialogue* (Cambridge, Mass.: Octagon Books, 1958), 277.

3 Andersen, *I retorikkens hage*, 67.

to broaden, particularize, and sharpen *style* as a critical instrument and a conceptual framework.

On entering the territory of rhetorical figures, at least two points that have already been made are worth reiterating. The first relates to W. G. Müller's identification of *elocutio* with the topos of style as dress. This was implied in an article published some twenty years after his book *Topik des Stilbegriffs*, in which style in the elocutionary tradition is viewed as grounded in a perception of language as something added to idea and content. This identification may, however, be challenged for its simplicity and criticized for suppressing the intermediate moves of history. It is likely to be contested by historians and critics of rhetoric who view the five parts as a coherent whole, whereas an unfortunate and unsettling separation of the parts are taken to be a later event, something which takes place in the course of history. [4] Viewed through the lenses of constitutive rhetoric and style, it is the theory of *officia oratoris* itself, the very division into five duties or parts, which installs the perception of language and style as a supplement to argumentation and thought. From this perspective, the conclusion arrived at by Müller seems both compelling and warranted.

Secondly, Müller argued that during the nineteenth century, this view lost ground to the Romantic topos of style as the incarnation of the speaker's personality. This thesis, however, is not quite steadfast. By default, the massive resistance to the topos of style as dress by prominent modern and late modern critics seems to indicate as much. That the notion of style as dress has not evaporated entirely is witnessed by some of the treatises on rhetorical figures – by, among others, I. A. Richards, George Lakoff, and Jeanne Fahnestock – discussed in

4 Fahnestock, for one, ascribes the separation of rhetorical figures from argumentation to "accidents of history" and the pedagogical practice of centuries past. Instead of viewing the canonical division as generative of a separation of form and content, she admits that it "translates too easily into a chronological sequence so that it is assumed to represent steps in the process of composition." Jeanne Fahnestock, *Rhetorical Figures in Science* (Oxford: Oxford University Press, 2002), 31.

the following pages: theories unanimously and explicitly written in opposition to this view.[5]

My investigation takes its starting point in Gérard Genette's bewitching depiction of rhetoric's historical reduction to style and figures. On a general level, of course, the picture he painted changed with the influence of *The New Rhetoric* and the growth of rhetorical criticism. More specifically, Perelman and Olbrechts-Tyteca reestablished rhetorical figures in the context of rhetoric, and rhetoric in the context of argumentation. Although their attention to the function of rhetorical figures charted a new course, some aspects of their defining moves need further critical scrutiny. In addition to my own points of objection, I account for the American rhetorical critic Jeanne Fahnestock's critique of some of the explications in *The New Rhetoric*. The discussion is followed by a presentation of her thesis that rhetorical figures are condensed arguments. Furthermore, I juxtapose her rhetorical approach with some modern theories of metaphor and discuss how they relate to the theory of style. Finally, the conceptual developments of the function and significance of rhetorical figures and style are furthered in a rhetorical criticism study of a Danish newspaper controversy about the rhetorical perspectives of the language used in hip hop lyrics.

5 A more detailed account of Richards' and Fahnestock's objections follows. As for Lakoff's opposition to the traditional view of figurative language as dress, the following quotation serves as an apt example: "In classical theories of language, metaphor was seen as a matter of language, not thought. Metaphorical expressions were assumed to be mutually exclusive with the realm of ordinary everyday language." George Lakoff, "The contemporary theory of metaphor," in *Metaphor and Thought*, ed. Andrew Ortony (Cambridge: Cambridge University Press, 1993), 202. Unlike Lakoff and Richards, Fahnestock does not reduce all Classical rhetoric to this view, as I shall elaborate below.

Stylistic Dominion

In "La rhétorique restreinte," the French literary critic Gérard Genette outlines how rhetoric has been exposed to one reduction after another.[6] In Antiquity, and namely in Aristotle's work, rhetoric consisted broadly of argumentation, style and delivery, but from the Middle Ages and on, a gradual displacement reduced rhetoric to *elocutio* and to a theory of rhetorical figures. This reductive process continued in French Neoclassical theories, where the substitution was the defining criteria of the whole field of rhetorical figures, and the trope became the model of all other rhetorical figures. Additional trimming and unifying resulted in what Genette announces to be the irreplaceable china dogs of our own modern rhetoric: metaphor and metonymy.[7] Finally, rhetoric reaches the last stage of the reduction process when metaphor swallows its fiercest opponent and ends up as a kind of 'figure of the figures', identical with rhetoric itself.

Since Genette's article, the tendency to focus on one, or a few, rhetorical figures has not exactly abated. Even though it is not the primary topic of my investigation, I shall in the present chapter look into some of these theories, especially those that have defined the contemporary research field of metaphor. I will, however, pass more lightly over the theories that imagine a fixed set of rhetorical figures to hold the power of exhaustive explanation. I shall briefly explain why.

The theories in question, mostly literary but also occasionally rooted in other academic fields, select a few rhetorical figures – be it two (metaphor and metonymy) or four (metaphor, metonymy, synecdoche and irony) – on which they build large theoretical schemes. With little sensitivity to the tangled and diffuse character of rhetorical figures in the rhetorical tradition, they ascribe to the figures a systematic rigor better suited to modern structuralism. A distinct example and pioneer

---

6 Gérard Genette, "La rhétorique restreinte," in *Communications* 16, *Recherches rhétoriques* (1994).

7 Ibid., 237.

work in this tradition is Roman Jakobson's study of two types of aphasia indicative of two fundamental principles of language: combination and selection. The polar opposition is, supposedly, universal; not only is it the organizing principle behind literary genres and periods (metaphor of poetry, Romanticism, and Symbolism; metonymy of prose and realism), it also "appears to be of primal significance and consequence for all verbal behavior and for human behavior in general."[8]

Similarly, I am hesitant of theories that originate from an idea of so-called 'master-tropes,' as well as the sort of schematics they result in. An example from outside the immediate realm of literary and rhetorical scholarship is the American historian Hayden White's application of four rhetorical figures to historiography. Although I share his premise that history itself does not have a structure, and only the language through which events become history does, I am not convinced that any theory based on a fixed set of categories suffices to provide knowledge and understanding of the narrative strategies available to history writing.[9] Especially since, in White's work, the four tropes – metaphor, metonymy, synecdoche, and irony – are part of a larger system of combined categories and classifications.

More precisely, I caution a certain high-strung ambition in the approach to rhetorical figures that fueled some structuralist and post-structuralist theories in the late twentieth century. As stated in the previous chapter, however, my critique of misapprehension of the rhetorical tradition is not meant as a general rejection of the theoretical foundation of these theories. On a more general level, I share their interest in thinking about sign and meaning, as well as the overall view on this relationship.

Certainly, this very interest appears to be the driving force behind Genettes' own investigation. Sooner than a mere depiction of how

8 Roman Jakobson, "Two Aspects of Language and Two Types of Aphasic Disturbances," in *Selected Writings II* (The Hague: Mouton, 1971), 256.

9 Hayden White, *Metahistory. The Historical Imagination in Nineteenth-Century Europe* (Baltimore: The Johns Hopkins University Press, 1973).

some parts of rhetoric went missing, Genette's errand may be captured as a socio-psychological critique of the reductive process and its almost ideological favoring of 'tropological' or metaphorical qualities such as quasi-identity (substitution) and pseudo-spatial presence. Genette pinpoints how our conception of language is based on a systematic preference for some qualities and also how this preference is concealed by seemingly neutral, or natural, rationalizations.[10] Thus, one may add, in the theoretical discussion of sign and meaning, Genette is not above using the limited outlook of a binary opposition.

As Genette also points out, this slightly caricatured draft of rhetoric's gradual emaciation offers too narrow a focus. He mentions several works which oppose the reductive development, one of which is the article "Rhétorique l'ancienne" by the French literary critic Roland Barthes. Barthes' article, which was published in the same issue of the journal *Communications*, aims at making rhetoric a model theory for modern mass communication by recollecting the dynamics of its detailed network.[11] It also includes what is absent from Genette's own list of references, namely the work which is often ascribed to having initiated rhetoric's revival in the twentieth century, *La Nouvelle Rhétorique* (1958) – or *The New Rhetoric*, as was the title of the translation which canonized the treatise in American rhetorical scholarship.[12] Its authors, the Belgians Chaïm Perelman and Lucie Olbrecths-Tyteca, define argumentation as distinct from demonstration and formal logic. Rhetorical argumentation does not take place within a closed system, nor does its conclusion arrive at truth in any absolute sense. Instead, it seeks the adherence of an audience based on premises of communal values and consensus.

10 Genette, "La rhétorique restreinte," 252.

11 Roland Barthes, "L'ancienne rhétorique. Aide-mémoire," in, *Communications* 16, *Recherches rhétoriques* (1994).

12 Chaïm Perelman & Lucie Olbrechts-Tyteca, *The New Rhetoric. A Treatise on Argumentation* (Notre Dame: University of Notre Dame Press, 1969).

Argumentative Figures in The New Rhetoric

More than twenty years after the publication of *The New Rhetoric*, Chaïm Perelman, in the first chapter of *The New Rhetoric and the Humanities* (1979), describes "the stylistic tradition of rhetoric" as having "hindered, and to a large extent actually destroyed, the tradition of ancient rhetoric that had been developed over the course of twenty centuries."[13] Undisputedly, *The New Rhetoric* constitutes a significant countermove to the theories which reduce rhetoric to a theory of style, but even so, Perelman and Olbrecht-Tyteca take their opposition to a restrained rhetoric further than seems warranted or useful. Their restitution of rhetoric as a theory of argumentation not only turns style into something subordinate to argumentation; in their new, and narrow, definition, style is actually exorcised from rhetoric!

Olbrechts-Tyteca and Perelman view rhetorical figures as part of the larger theory of argumentation which aims to induce or increase adherence in an audience. In the context of argumentation, rhetorical figures are interesting only in so far as they bring about a new perspective. The authors sketch how the perception of argumentative figures takes place. At first, one has to recognize a rhetorical figure as a discernable structure, a form and a use that differs from normal usage and, consequently, attracts attention.[14] From then on, the figure may either succeed as an argumentative figure, or fail. As a result of the authors' argumentation agenda, the more technical distinction between tropes and figures inherited from traditional rhetoric is left behind. Instead, they introduce a functional distinction between *argumentative figures* and *figures of style*. In this framework, a figure obtains argumentative status when the initial distinction between normal and abnormal usage is dissolved through the effect that the speech produces. In the interpretative process, the original figure, distinctive because of an

13 Chaïm Perelman, *The New Rhetoric and the Humanities* (Dordrecht: D. Reidel Publishing Company, 1979), 2.

14 Perelman & Olbrechts-Tyteca, *The New Rhetoric*, 168.

anomaly in relation to normal usage, now comes to appear normal because its use is justified by the speech taken as a whole.[15]

However, if the rhetorical figure fails to produce a new perspective or gain the adherence of an audience, it cannot aspire to be more than a figure of style, an ornament bereft of any argumentative function:

> We consider a figure to be *argumentative*, if it brings about a change of perspective, and its use seems normal in relation to this new situation. If, on the other hand, the speech does not bring about the adherence of the hearer to this argumentative form, the figure will be considered an embellishment, a figure of style. It can excite admiration, but this will be on the aesthetic plane, or in recognition of the speaker's originality.[16]

As conceptualized by Perelman and Olbrechts-Tyteca, style is argumentation's radical 'Other': Figures of style may produce sentiments like admiration or pleasure, but that does not count as an effect of argumentation.

Like most things in their theory of rhetoric, Olbrecht-Tyteca and Perelman's distinction between argumentative figures and figures of style depends on the audience. The judgment of the argumentative function of rhetorical figures relies on the audience's perception:

> In order to perceive its argumentative aspect, it is necessary to conceive of a step from the common to the uncommon, and a return to another order of commonness [...]. Further, and this is perhaps the most important point, it is necessary to understand that the normal expression is relative not only to a milieu, an audience, but to a particular moment in the discourse.[17]

---

15 Ibid., 169.

16 Ibid.

17 Ibid., 171.

According to the authors of *The New Rhetoric* it would, therefore, be a mistake to say that a given figure, recognizable because of its formal structure, will always produce the same effect in argumentation. The function of a figure is not something static; it is always dependent on the context. As a consequence, *The New Rhetoric* presents the rhetorical figures quite differently from most manuals of rhetoric. Instead of an elaborated account of each figure's formal structure and persuasive effect, Olbrechts-Tyteca and Perelman emphasize that the figures are to be examined in their argumentative context. In their own investigation, a few rhetorical figures are grouped and presented according to argumentative purposes: figures that impose or suggest a choice (for instance *periphrasis* or *correctio*), figures that increase the feeling of presence (for instance *anaphora or onomatopoeia*), or figures that increase communion with the audience (for instance *allusion*). Apart from this preliminary sorting, specific rhetorical figures are also taken up in the course of the general treatment of different aspects of argumentation.

Whereas Genette's description of rhetoric centers on a diminution to style and rhetorical figures, the rhetoric of Perelman and Olbrechts-Tyteca is 'whole', inclusive, and has an argumentative basis. If we recall the discussion in chapter one, their distinction between argumentative figures and figures of style resembles the two topoi essential to Müller's theory of style. According to this parallel, Perelman and Olbrechts-Tyteca's idea of argumentative figures comes close to the description of style as the incarnation of thought and argument, whereas their idea of figures of style approaches the description of style as dress. Contrary to Müller's understanding, however, Perelman and Olbrechts-Tyteca's binary opposition is used to a normative end which expels the latter topos from rhetoric. Their rehabilitation of rhetoric as a substantial theory of argumentation reestablishes it within an ethical realm where communication is judged in the light of its social and moral values and, accordingly, rhetorical figures are judged in the light of their argumentative function.

Redefining Rhetorical Figures

The French philosopher Olivier Reboul has contested the separation of feeling and argumentation that is a consequence of Olbrechts-Tyteca and Perelman's explanation of rhetorical figures. In his view, they fail to explain the pleasure or delight that rhetorical figures can excite, for instance through humor. "The essence of rhetoric is to not distinguish feeling from understanding. This is why a figure is stronger than the argument it condenses."[18] On par with modern theories of metaphor, Reboul understands metaphors to be more than arguments through analogy. [19]

The treatment of rhetorical figures in *The New Rhetoric* has also been criticized by the American rhetorical critic Jeanne Fahnestock. Arguing from the perspective of rhetoric as a coherent whole in five parts, she acknowledges that the authors have recovered the relation between *inventio* and rhetorical figures. Meanwhile, her reservations regarding their definitions of the figures are strong. Above all, she finds it problematic that the figures should be linked to a psychological experience where the audience becomes attentive to a word or an expression and then allegedly accepts it because of its efficiency as an argument. She also criticizes the idea that the argumentative potential of rhetorical figures should depend on how noticeable they are, as well as that the audience's ability to recognize a figure should count as a norm for whether the figure exists or not.

In *Rhetorical Figures in Science* (1999), Jeanne Fahnestock redefines rhetorical figures in a conceptual, critical discussion from which I will excerpt key points here. As the title of the book clearly indicates, her primary topic is rhetorical figures in scientific texts. I comment on the theoretical implications of this topic in brief before I account for Fahnestock's argument on rhetoric and rhetorical figures and the

18 Olivier Reboul, "The Figure and the Argument," in *From Metaphysics to Rhetoric*, ed. Michel Meyer (Dordrecht: Kluwer Academic Publishers, 1989), 178.

19 Ibid. Thus, Reboul understands Olbrechts-Tyteca's *Le comique de discours* (1974) as a necessary corrective to the too rational *The New Rhetoric*.

perspectives it entails. According to Fahnestock, her study of rhetorical figures in science aims at reestablishing the connection between the separated cultures of rhetoric and science. As such, it seeks to correct the assumption that no rhetorical figures – except for the metaphor – have ever played a role in scientific discourse. Her study proves that rhetorical figures can be found everywhere, and it demonstrates the continuity of the structure of reasoning across traditionally separated disciplines. From that, it follows that the poetical metaphor cannot be essentially different from the metaphor used in scientific thinking.[20]

Fahnestock's investigation takes its critical outset in a definition of rhetorical figures as a deviation from normal usage. In terms of stylistic topoi, an understanding of style as dress is clearly at its center. Fahnestock suggests Quintilian was the first to view rhetorical figures as a departure from a register presumably more common or normal, and she demands an explanation of what 'normal usage' might be.[21] Yet this explanation has never been given, and it cannot be given in any satisfactory way.

To Fahnestock, all theories that define rhetorical figures as a departure – whether they are supposed to have left a more acceptable, common, or 'simple' usage – are based on the assumption that the figure is a substitution for another linguistic choice.[22] This assumption rests on an implicit and unfortunate separation of the language into two domains, a literal and a figurative. In the conclusion to her thorough historical research, Fahnestock groups all the definitions that

20 Nevertheless, Fahnestock emphasizes that her own project is not another study that wishes to topple science from its "epistemologically superior position." On the contrary, she understands the difference between science and other fields as substantial, although it depends less on the forms of arguments used than on the degree of accountability demanded of the practical output: For natural science that accountability is high, and there is more pressure to turn an argument into prediction or action. Ibid., 43.

21 Ibid, 15. This view is adopted by, among others, Henry Peacham in 1593 and Jean Paulhan in 1953. Ibid.

22 Fahnestock, *Rhetorical Figures in Science*, 17.

explain rhetorical figures as sources of feeling, charm, vividness, force, or elegance in one category which she characterizes as *value-added* theories of figuration.[23] According to the theory of value addition, rhetorical figures add some aesthetic, emotional, or persuasive quality which enhances the effect. This understanding, in turn, implies a non-figured language domain: "But if they 'add to,' of course, they can also be 'subtracted from.' Anyone holding to a 'value-added' theory of the figures is also likely to believe, at least by default, in an unfigured or degree-zero style."[24]

Fahnestock provides an elaborated example of this line of reasoning which she admits seems to some degree sensible enough. For instance, it seems possible to translate a passage of 'figured' text into a 'literal' register: "Alas! Gone are the daisies of summer" can become "Unfortunately summer is over". The first, 'figured' version displays more figures, for instance an exclamation in the form of an *ekpronesis* (*exclamatio*) and a syntactical inversion with *hyperbaton*, as well as the metonymy "daisies of summer" for summer itself. The other version displays none of the devices known from the manuals of rhetorical figures.

Still, Fahnestock regards the value-added theories to be a misunderstanding. She challenges their theoretical basis by asking whether the feelings that are presumably added by the use of rhetorical figures can also be expressed without identifiable figures. The example from above can be rephrased into what seems to be a matter-of-fact statement, deprived of any emotion: "It is September 22". But this sentence can

23 In this respect, Fahnestock cuts through the discussions in the beginning of this chapter about the correct perception of *ornatus* as associated with strength rather than beauty and emotion: "Comparing the *exornationes* to armament rather than to decoration certainly endows them with greater power and efficacy. But both meanings keep the figures on the surface where they can be readily removed; even Homer's heroes can be stripped of their weapons and armor when they fall." Fahnestock, *Rhetorical Figures in Science*, 19.

24 Ibid.

easily be interpreted to contain emotion since meaning depends on the contextual appearance: "The execution is set for September 23rd. It is September 22."[25]

The value-added theories can also be refuted by simply asking whether it is possible to say anything, 'figured' or not, without emotion. Even the most 'simple' or 'direct' sentence, like "It is September 22," can be said to add feelings, for instance of seriousness, calmness, or strong conviction. And, if it is impossible to have a text without emotion, it cannot at the same time be said that rhetorical figures add feelings where no feelings were found at the outset; they simply help to express the feelings appropriate in the context.[26]

Fahnestock finds that the value-added theories are misleading because they have mistakenly reinforced a division in language between two domains.[27] In another analytical example concerning the rhetorical figure *aposiopesis*, she criticizes the idea that feelings can be subtracted from an utterance so that only the 'content' is left. Fahnestock's example is: "And then he read in the letter that ..." The abrupt breaking off of an utterance before it has been completed presumably conveys the speaker's sudden emotional breakdown. The cause of the interruption – the content of the letter is too offensive, too horrible, or too revealing – can perhaps be found in the context. But the *aposiopesis* also tells the reader that there is something that the speaker will not, or cannot, say. A speaker could have obtained the same effect by saying "I cannot say what he read in the letter." But the abruption and the dangling, half sentence delivers this same content iconically: The sentence does what it says.[28]

To Fahnestock, this example illustrates that it serves no purpose to make a distinction between two separate domains in language. Instead it is much more useful to regard the means available for any

25 Ibid., 21.

26 Ibid.

27 Ibid., 22.

28 Ibid.

given function as a series of possibilities. These possibilities cannot be separated into different levels, a 'figurative' and a 'literal':

> Instead, the choices available to a speaker can be thought of as less to more constitutive or iconic. The figures of speech occupy examined territory on this continuum of expressive possibilities. They have traditionally been used (and hence identified) as particularly effective ways of saying what can also be said in many other ways. They are, in other words, ideally but not exclusively constitutive of a text's many meanings, simply doing better what it is possible to do with other means, or even doing best what they are traditionally identified as doing.[29]

It follows that it cannot be decided once and for all what will be the most appropriate expression. The concrete situation dictates whether it would be best to use a rhetorical figure. The enactment of the *aposiopesis* is the strongest choice for expressing that something is inexpressible, but that does not mean that it will always be the most effective way. It is possible to imagine situations where it would be a wiser rhetorical choice to state "I cannot/will not say what he read in that letter."[30]

In sum, practical as well as theoretical implications follow from Fahnestock's redefinition of rhetorical figures. By thinking of rhetorical figures as better, but not unique, ways to obtain certain discursive functions, she manages to maneuver away from some of the difficulties of definition that have troubled the field. This enables her, firstly, to account for why a valid theoretical explanation of the separation between figurative language and 'un-figured,' 'normal' usage has never been given. Secondly, it offers her a way out of the defining difficulties:

29 Ibid.

30 Ibid., 23.

> The figures may be at once acceptable usage and statistically atypical usage as well as carriers of emotion and vividness and force. They can be said to "add distinction" or other virtues in the sense that the text with appropriate figures has used the most effective linguistic means possible to do its work. Even the mechanism of substitution can be retained, so long as it means reaching into the same bag for different choices, not into an opposite sort of bag. None of these descriptions is incompatible with a more precise characterization of the figures as the formal embodiments of certain ideational or persuasive functions.[31]

The task of rationalizing, of sorting out the differing contradictory definitions of rhetorical figures, in Fahnestock's view becomes superfluous. Thus, it may be acceptable to say that rhetorical figures 'add' feelings, vividness or force, as long as the choice is perceived as a difference in degree within the same language paradigm, and not between fundamentally distinct discursive registers.

In my view, however, the conceptual inclusiveness that Fahnestock invites here runs the risk of bringing about theoretical confusion. It is puzzling that Fahnestock, whose own artillery has been directed at the topos style as dress, should welcome terms and metaphors that are likely to reinstate this perception. According to other parts of her thinking on rhetorical figures, a specific formulation would constitute a specific argument. Therefore, a change of metaphor should follow a change of perception.

Figures as Epitomized Arguments

The prime subject of Fahnestock's investigation is a handful of figures that can be identified as certain lines of argumentation or reasoning.

31 Ibid.

In the rhetorical tradition, some rhetorical figures have been associated with the general lines in reasoning known as *topoi*. It is an undisputed truth that the metaphor is the epitome of analogical reasoning, but in Fahnestock's view, this insight could easily be expanded to other figures: "One need only accept that human reasoning exploits more than analogy, and that, therefore, more figures than metaphor are linked to corresponding modes of reasoning."[32]

The *antimetabole* is an apt example of a figure which is an epitome of an argument. The definition of this figure is that it reverses the relative positions of key terms in parallel phrases. Fahnestock has found a perfect example in an advertisment from the 1950s for cellophane wrapping: "Protects what it shows/Shows what it protects." The reversal of the pair of key terms when they are repeated, "protects" and "shows", makes a pithy argument for the product. This new material possesses two interchangeable and simultaneous qualities; it makes the food both safe and visible. A rhetorical figure will often be used along with an expanded version of the argument which provides the details that back up the central claim made by the figure. It is an important point that the rhetorical figure is the argument in its most condensed form: "In the presence of more text, it could be said, as the old manuals would put it, that the precise phrasing of this figure adds force or vividness to the whole argument. But it also is the argument itself in the most compressed form possible. If the text were to be reduced to one sentence, that one sentence, emblematic of the whole, would be the figure."[33]

Fahnestock's further investigation evolves as a study of primarily four rhetorical figures which have traditionally been associated with the structural thinking known as reasoning or argumentation: *antithesis*, *incrementum* (and *gradatio*), *antimetabole*, and *ploche* (and *polyptoton*).[34] Some conceptual and methodological perspectives fol-

---

32 Ibid., 24.

33 Ibid., 25.

34 Fahnestock investigates a larger stylistic territory in *Rhetorical Style. The Uses of Language in Persuasion* (Oxford: Oxford University Press, 2011).

low from the definition of figures as certain durable lines in the argumentation. When rhetorical figures are perceived as epitomes of a longer line of argument, the argumentation may persist even when it is not epitomized in an iconic form. The analytical and critical focus therefore changes from the rigid definition of what figures 'are' to a description of their argumentative function. Furthermore, Fahnestock is not afraid to talk about an argument, for instance *antithesis* or *gradatio*, although the figure only appears in half-finished form:

> But an argument need not be epitomized, need not be expressed succinctly. It can be phrased and paraphrased in wordier ways. The argument survives though the figure, as some of the passages cited in the following chapters will demonstrate. Darwin, for example, was not above interrupting a gradation for a sentence of clarifying definition [...]. He and so many other more recent authors "relax" the figures from their purest forms into near-figures. They do not epitomize their arguments perfectly, perhaps fearing that the epitome may be too noticeable, too bold a foregrounding of the form of an argument.[35]

As a result, Fahnestock is able to define rhetorical figures as epitomes of reasoning structures and still accept the existence of a figure when the wording is looser, i.e. when the epitome is missing. In this respect, her explanation is analogous to Müller's understanding of topology as 'double natured': It refers both to the 'underlying' central argument and thought and to the exact phrasing. To illustrate this, Fahnstock compares it to the more familiar problem of metaphor: "A metaphor can be spread throughout a text in an extended analogy or allegory; it can provide a principle of organization in an extended comparison, or it can be succinctly expressed in a single word choice. It can even take all these forms in the same text. Or one can find

35 Fahnestock, *Rhetorical Figures in Science*, 40.

the reasoning epitomized by the figure without necessarily finding the figure itself."[36]

As a consequence, Fahnestock moves her attention from the definition of rhetorical figures to the analysis of the argumentative or reasoning function. This functional perspective enables her to discuss and analyze the *structure* of a given rhetorical figure; that is, its basic argumentative lines, its topics. The interest in the more general lines of how and with what purpose a figure can be used takes the investigation in the direction of a constitutive function of rhetorical figures. From this perspective, rhetorical figures are more than effective means to enhance an argument or bring attention to content which is already there. Instead, they are seen as constitutive of the very idea or topic treated.

Fahnestock finds an example of this in Charles Darwin's *On the Origin of Species* (1859), where he uses an argumentative strategy aimed at breaking down the differences between fixed categories. Darwin reasons though the figure *gradatio* when he undermines the notion of stable species by pointing toward the many smaller differences existing among individuals of a certain species.[37] In Fahnestock's words: "Species are graded into subspecies, subspecies into varieties, varieties into individual differences, and these in turn "blend" insensibly. The result is a smooth continuum rather than rigidly partitioned categories."[38]

That rhetorical figures can be precise and effective arguments, or lines of reasoning, is a thesis which Fahnestock shares with some other theorists of rhetoric. As an alternative to the value-added theories, she traces a rhetorical tradition consisting of works by Aristotle, Cicero, Hermogenes, Melanchton, Sister Miriam Joseph, Kenneth Burke, and Perelman and Olbrechts-Tyteca. In viewing rhetorical figures as ideational and essential to reason and argumentation, these rhetorical

36 Ibid., 41.

37 *Gradatio* is a climbing argument with *anadiplosis*, which repeats the close of one sentence in the opening of the next.

38 Ibid., 113-115.

thinkers presaged her own investigations' perception of language and thought.

Modern Theories of Metaphor

Like Genette, Fahnestock regrets it when the study of rhetoric is restricted to metaphor alone, but she specifically blames metaphor for stealing the attention from the larger repertoire of rhetorical figures. Because her study covers argumentation and reason in rhetorical figures *other* than metaphor, it passes lightly over theories of metaphor. Still, obvious parallels between my discussion of style, Fahnestock's theory of rhetorical figures, and the theories of metaphor should not be overlooked. Over the next few pages, I consider the disputes and arguments about addition, substitution, interaction, and mapping that have been central to theories of metaphor, both modern and old. The theoretical exploration concludes with a return to Fahnestock's alternative theory, and subsequently to the problem of style, notably constitutive style.

One of the first leading figures in the field of research devoted to metaphor is the literary critic I. A. Richards, who defines his interest in rhetoric broadly as the study of understanding and misunderstanding. In a move characteristic of the stylistic tradition summarized by Genette, Richards takes the metaphor to be at the center of rhetoric. Richards regards his own conception of rhetoric to be a revision of the Classical rhetorical theories that were based on a distinction between a literal, proper level and the figural, transferred level.

He refers to Aristotle's observation in *Poetics* that it takes a certain kind of talent to master a metaphor: "It is the one thing that cannot be learnt from others; and it is also a sign of genius, since a good metaphor implies an intuitive perception of the similarity in dissimilars."[39]

---

39 Aristotle, *Poetics* in *The Basic Works of Aristotle*, ed. Richard McKeon (New York: The Modern Library, 2001), 1459a.

This remark has led to the assumption that metaphor is something special and extraordinary in language, a deviation from normal usage:

> Throughout the history of Rhetoric, metaphor has been treated as a sort of happy extra trick with words, an opportunity to exploit the accidents of their versatility, something in place occasionally but requiring unusual skill and caution. In brief, a grace or ornament or *added* power of language, not its constitutive form.[40]

But to Richards, this assumption is misleading. The problem is that it understands metaphor as a replacement and that it focuses on words alone: "And thereby it made metaphor seem to be a verbal matter, a shifting and displacement of words, whereas fundamentally it is a borrowing between and intercourse of thoughts, a transaction between contexts."[41]

Richards perceives metaphor as an interaction of contexts, and he introduces the terms *tenor* and *vehicle* to describe this collaboration between the content and the carrier of meaning. The important point is that the interaction between tenor and vehicle generates a new meaning: "the co-presence of the vehicle and tenor results in a meaning (to be clearly distinguished from the tenor) which is not attainable without their interaction."[42]

In Richards' redefinition, metaphor becomes something more than the analogy that Aristotles considered it to be, because it cannot be

40 I. A. Richards, *The Philosophy of Rhetoric* (London: Oxford University Press, 1936), 90.

41 Ibid., 94.

42 According to Richards, the influence of the interaction varies a great deal: "At one extreme the vehicle may become almost a mere decoration or coloring of the tenor, at the other extreme, the tenor may become almost a mere excuse for the introduction of the vehicle, and so no longer be 'the principal subject.'" Ibid., 100.

translated 'back' without a loss of meaning. In *Poetics*, Aristotle defines metaphor as follows: "Metaphor is the movement of an alien word from either genus to species or from species to genus or from species to species or by analogy."[43] The metaphor based on analogy he defines thus: "I call it analogy when the second thing is related to the first as the fourth is to the third; for [a poet] will say the fourth for the second or the second for the fourth."[44] One of Aristotle's examples is that old age is to life as evening is to day: "Or since old age is to life as evening is to day, then he will call evening the old age of day or, like Empedocles, call old age the evening of life or 'life's gloaming.'"[45]

In *On Rhetoric*, Aristotle juxtaposes the metaphor and the *simile*, a juxtaposition that is also found in Quintilian's definition of metaphor as a substitution: "On the whole *metaphor* is a shorter form of *simile*, while there is this further difference, that in the latter we compare some object to the thing which we wish to describe, whereas in the former this object is actually substituted for the thing. It is a comparison when I say that a man did something *like a lion*, it is a metaphor when I say of him, *He is a lion*."[46]

In *The New Rhetoric*, Perelman and Olbrecht-Tyteca reassert the analogy as paradigm for the metaphor when they define metaphor as a condensed analogy. But the authors leave the notion of substitution behind when they adhere to Richard's understanding of metaphor as interaction: "In the context of argumentation, at least, we cannot better describe a metaphor than by conceiving it as a condensed analogy, resulting from the fusion of an element from the phoros with an element from the theme."[47]

---

43 Aristotle, *Poetics* in *On Rhetoric. A Theory of Civic Discourse*, trans. George A. Kennedy (Oxford: Oxford University Press), 1457b.

44 Ibid.

45 Ibid.

46 Quintilian, *The Instituio Oratoria of Quintilian I–IV* (The Loeb Classical Library, 1953), VIII.6.8.

47 Perelman & Olbrechts-Tyteca, *The New Rhetoric*, 399.

Richard's theory about the metaphor as interaction is taken up and developed by, among others, philosophers like Max Black and Paul Ricoeur; these ideas are often grouped and characterized as "theories of interaction." The critique of the notion of substitution found in (some) Classical theories of rhetoric is of focal concern to the theorists of interaction who think of metaphorical interaction as a production of meaning. In his summary of theories of metaphor in Aristotle, Cicero, and Quintilian, Paul Ricoeur stresses that in Classical rhetoric, the transported term was not considered to be a semantic renewal, since "it is possible to translate a metaphor, i.e. restore the literal meaning that the figurative word is a substitution for."[48]

As observed by Max Black, theories of metaphorical substitution are simply particular discussions taking place within a general understanding of rhetorical figures as a deviation from normal or literal language.[49] Theories of interaction leave behind the idea that the metaphor brings about a 1:1 change of meaning and that it can be transported back with no loss of meaning. To Max Black, the metaphor is an interaction between two systems, a primary and a secondary. In the juxtaposition, the associations related to the secondary system are projected towards the primary subject that it organizes. Meanwhile, it follows from the theory of interaction that both systems are influenced.[50] Black's theoretical framework is generally consistent with Richards', yet it gains distinction by some elaborated examples, such as "The poor are the negroes of Europe":

> The substitution view, at its crudest, tells us that something is being indirectly said about the poor of Europe. (But what? That they are an oppressed class, a standing reproach to the

48 Paul Ricoeur, *Fortolkningsteori* (København: Vinten, 1979), 167. My translation.

49 Max Black, *Models and Metaphors. Studies in Language and Philosophy* (Ithaca: Cornell University Press, 1972), 35.

50 Max Black, "More about Metaphor," in *Metaphor and Thought*, ed. Andrew Ortony (Cambridge: Cambridge University Press, 1993), 27-28.

community's official ideals, that poverty is inherited and indelible?) The comparison view claims that the epigram presents some comparison between the poor and the negroes. In opposition to both, Richards says that our "thoughts" about European poor and American negroes are "active together" and "interact" to produce a meaning that is a resultant of that interaction. I think this must mean that in the given context the focal word "negroes" obtains a new meaning in literal uses, not quite the meaning which any literal substitute would have.[51]

The tendency to study ordinary language usage and focus on general and common discursive processes is intensified by the cognitive semantic theories. Their primary foci are the so-called conventional metaphors that can be found everywhere in the language and are usually not recognized as metaphors. The cognitive semantic view on metaphor explicitly defies Classical rhetorical theories that conceive of metaphor and other rhetorical figures as departures from normal usage. Conversely, the cognitive linguistics George Lakoff and Mark Johnson understand metaphor as pervasive in everyday life: not just in language, but also in thought and action.[52] According to the cognitive theory of metaphors, the ordinary conceptual system is fundamentally metaphorical.

By analyzing metaphorical linguistic expressions such as "We're at a crossroad," "We can't turn back now," or "I don't think this relationship is going anywhere," one can understand how human thought processes are structured metaphorically.[53] In the theoretical vocabulary of cognitive linguistics, however, metaphors do not appear in language, but are a kind of conceptual system that structures perceptive domains in relation to each other.

51 Black, *Models and Metaphors*, 38-39.

52 George Lakoff & Mark Johnson, *Metaphors We Live By* (Chicago: The University of Chicago Press, 1980), 3.

53 Ibid., 44.

The metaphorical expressions mentioned above all belong to the metaphorical concept "Love is a journey," which does not exist in language, but is something one can deduce from the most commonly used metaphorical expressions. Other familiar metaphors in our cultural context are, for instance, "Argument is war," "Time is money," "Life is a journey," or the so-called orientational metaphors that organize whole conceptual systems. Orientational metaphors often draw on a spatial structuring of concepts, for instance, "Happy is up," which leads to expressions like "You're in high spirits," or, conversely, "I'm feeling down."[54]

The orientational metaphors are especially apt for illustrating that metaphorical organization is part of everyday language. They are not likely to be noticed as metaphorical, nor will they be perceived as a deviation from a 'literal' discursive register. Lakoff defines metaphor as "a cross-domain mapping in the conceptual system,"[55] which is based on his and Mark Turner's distinction between two domains – a target domain that we want to understand, and a source domain which is the structure of the domain that we use to understand the target domain.

In *More than Cool Reason*, this definition is turned into a critique of the theories of interaction which believed the metaphors to influence both target and source:

> When we understand that life is a journey we structure life in terms of a journey, and map onto the domain of life the inferential structure associated with journeys. But we do not map onto the domain of journeys the inferential structure associated with the domain of life. For example, we do not understand thereby that journeys have waking and sleeping parts, as lives do. We do not infer that, just as we can lead

---

54 Ibid., 15.

55 George Lakoff, "The Contemporary Theory of Metaphor," 203.

only one life, so a traveler can take only one journey. We map one way only, from the source domain of journey onto the target domain of life.[56]

Although the cognitive approach differs from the theories of interaction that say the metaphors should work both ways, in other respects it comes quite close to the lines laid out by Richards. Richards has criticized the idea that metaphor should count as something special, which stands apart from ordinary usage. Later theories of interaction maintain this critique of the theories that advocate the notion of departure. To Max Black, the interaction between systems influences both systems and leads to a mutual re-organization. The metaphorical re-organization of associations results in new meanings that would not have existed without the metaphor. Or, simply put, the same could not have been said in other words.

Metaphor, Rhetorical Figures, and Style

There are more than a few significant similarities between the theories of metaphor and Fahnestock's theory about rhetorical figures as condensed arguments. Particularly conspicuous is the mutual dissociation from former theories' distinction between figurative and normal language – a dissociation perfectly summed up by Fahnestock's introduction of the alternative metaphor of reaching into one bag for different linguistic choices, instead of into two different bags. Similarly, a swift *tabula rasa* constitutes the modern theories of metaphor as a field of research. It is in their positioning against a construct of Classical rhetoric perceiving metaphor as an extraordinary quality that modern metaphor studies come to define themselves as a specific school of thought.

56 George Lakoff & Mark Turner, *More than Cool Reason* (Chicago: University of Chicago Press, 1989), 131-132.

Furthermore, the dissociation from the idea of substitution leads both Fahnestock and the metaphor theories to stress the productive and constitutive aspects of rhetorical figures. In the context of metaphor, the constructive aspect is inherent in the break with the substitution view. When metaphor is no longer thought of as a process of substitution, it may be recognized for its production of meaning. The litmus test will be whether or not it is possible to 'translate back', that is to restore the original, 'literal' meaning. If not, the metaphor has generated a new meaning. As previously noted, the battle over metaphor takes place in a particular corner of the wider battlefield over rhetorical figures. It follows that insight into the creative potential of metaphor synecdochally refutes the idea of rhetorical figures as unessential additions or deviations.

With still greater exactitude Fahnestock has countered the widespread view that rhetorical figures add some quality or value – be it beauty, feeling, or force – to the content. In the same way, this approach rests firmly on the idea of two fundamentally different registers of language, a literal and a figurative. And according to this view, in applying a rhetorical figure, one may add some quality or value to the argument, but the argument itself will remain the same. The litmus test of the value-added view will show that the removal of a rhetorical figure leaves the argument essentially unaltered.

In Fahnestock's interpretative frame, the realization that rhetorical figures are structural argumentation leads to a re-configuration of rhetorical figures from *elocutio* to *inventio*. However, when compared to the categories of style that I developed in chapter one, the theoretical implications of her comprehension are less certain. Obviously, Fahnestock and the theories of metaphor agree on a denial of the traditional understanding of style and rhetoric grounded in the topos of style as dress. In his interpretation of this topos, Müller was careful not to reduce it to surface, but emphasized how it was closely intertwined with social norms such as decorum, manners, and the rhetorical constraints of class. Even so, the topos still essentially adheres to an understanding of style as an added feature.

Having thoroughly argued her opposition to the misjudgment of style and rhetorical figures as dress, Fahnestock still leaves us with the question of how to perceive her alternative theory – especially in regard to my conceptualization of style, which intersects a division between a view of coherence and a view of constitution. Therefore, it remains to be decided whether Fahnestock's theory fits the topos of style as an incarnation of substance and thought, or whether it reaches out for a conception of style as constitutive of identity and rhetorical significance.

In a series of questions put forward in the introduction, she strives towards a constitutive view: "To what extent does language do our thinking for us? How do the structures or options available in a language lead us into certain prepared lines of thought or argument? This book also belongs in the genre of studies in the rhetoric of science, and it, too, concerns the generative power of language."[57] Likewise in her introduction, she emphasizes that "This work investigates the conceptual and inventive power of certain figures of speech other than metaphor and the tropes allied to metaphor, whose cognitive significance has been so thoroughly explored recently."[58] And her summary subscribes to the same prerogative of language: "In a general as well as a very particular sense, then, a style argues."[59]

However, elsewhere, Fahnestock's choice of words is in many ways congenial with Müller's essentially Romantic topos of style as the man. As a consequence of her interest in the cognitive and argumentative aspect of rhetorical figures (style as thought), she omits the aspect of individuality (style as man) favored in Müller's historical account. In the following example, she distinctly argues from within a dichotomy of the two familiar topoi, style as dress and style as the incarnation of thought: "It needs to be extended to the other figures so that they are no longer seen as decoration on the plain cloth of language but as the

---

57 Fahnestock, *Rhetorical Figures in Science*, vii.

58 Ibid., viii.

59 Ibid., xii.

fabric itself."[60] Similarly, a coherence of form and intent is inherent in these examples from chapter one: "As Edward Surtz put it, the whole art of elocution and the figures in the rhetorical tradition can be described as a search for 'the perfect expression for one's idea.'"[61] And: "None of these descriptions is incompatible with a more precise characterization of the figures as the formal embodiments of certain ideational or persuasive functions."[62]

Viewed through my suggested grid of three stylistic topoi, I can only draw the conclusion that Fahnestock swings to and fro between a perception of rhetorical figures as the incarnation of thought and argument and the bolder idea that reflective structures are created by rhetorical figures. At any rate, she neither distinguishes explicitly between the two epistemologies, nor reflects along the lines of such distinction.

A consideration of epistemological outlook has been preempted by one of her sources, who will have the final word before I turn to the perspectives of rhetorical analysis and criticism. In a short and suggestive study, James M. Murphy proposes a relation between topos and rhetorical figures, a relation that is now lost. But he imagines that the recovery of such a relationship would have many implications, which seem to depend upon the terminological premise:

> Implicit in this question of the relation of topos to the figura is an even more fundamental question which strikes to the epistemological roots of our Western linguistic history. The question is so fundamental that its phrasing is critical: to put the question in the jargon of post-Roman rhetorical terminology, is Invention the same as Style? To put it in Aristotelian terms, does thought precede language? To put it into post-Saussurean terms, is language the same as thought, or perhaps

60 Ibid., xi–xii.

61 Ibid., 22. Vickers, *In Defence of Rhetoric*, 283.

62 Fahnestock, *Rhetorical Figures in Science*, 23.

the creator of thought? To put it in post-Chomsky terms, is language capacity prior to thought and independent of it?[63]

Analyzing Hip Hop Style and Rhetorical Figures

Unlike style, rhetorical figures are appealing as analytical concepts because they are concrete, potent with meaning, and make up a large reservoir of ready and handy devices for the rhetorical critic to use in their analysis. More often than not, however, the critic or student experiences that the analysis of rhetorical figures does not reach its full potential. She may become stranded in the captive project of conceptual classification and never make it to the analysis. Or she may consult the manuals and glossaries at hand, only to be equipped with concepts rather weakly founded in theory. I shall attempt to avoid both pitfalls as I present rhetorical figures and style as significant analytical concepts that are part of a comprehensive theoretical complex.

In respect to rhetorical analysis, Fahnestock's study is of principal importance. Not only is her discussion not limited to metaphor or a few tropes; she also in practice widens the scope of academic research and engages in rhetoric's tradition of a much broader repertoire of rhetorical figures. And instead of making generalized claims about processes of experience and perception, she approaches the figures as rhetorical possibilities. It is therefore charged with an analytical potential that I shall soon release. Besides rhetorical figures, the reading also takes into consideration the critical aspects of rhetorical style.

What follows is a reading of argumentative discourse, a debate, which discusses and employs rhetorical figures and style argumentatively. It is a debate study, as well as study of a meta-debate. The first

---

63 James J. Murphy, "*Topos* and *Figura*: Historical cause and effect?", in *De Ortu Grammaticae. Studies in Medieval Grammar and Linguistic Theory in Memory of Jan Pinborg*, ed. G. L. Bursill-Hall et al. (Amsterdam: John Benjamins Publishing Company, 1990), 247.

text was written by the Danish journalist and novelist, Hanne-Vibeke Holst, and it was printed in the newspaper *Politiken* under the headline "You are Fucking Sexist, Niarn!"[64] It has the form of an open letter to the Danish rapper Niarn, bears the explanatory subtitle "Letter to a Gangsta Rapper," and opens accordingly with a "Dear Niarn!" Hanne-Vibeke Holst addresses the person she is attacking, the rapper Niarn, but it is not Niarn who is inscribed as the primary audience. Although the article has the appearance of a letter, the actual genre is debate. According to the Danish rhetorical critic, Charlotte Jørgensen, debaters do not address their arguments to each other, but to the audience: "The speakers are not supposed to convince each other, but seek approval for their viewpoints about the matter of dispute from the listening third party."[65] In fact, it is considered to be a violation of the genre if the debaters are persuaded by one another:

> The purpose is not that the debaters come to agree; they are supposed to put forward their standpoints in order for a third party, on this basis, to make a decision. For this reason, it is not part of the 'contract' that the debaters should be willing to be persuaded in relation to the main claim.[66]

This golden rule applies especially to formalized types of debate such as television panel debates, which have a clear-cut distribution of roles and a fixed timetable. But it also goes for debates that are more complex in structure, for instance those taking place in newspapers. They are often quite unpredictable in terms of structure and duration; for instance, they may be prolonged, as different aspects of a complex situation each become the center of the discussion.

---

64 Hanne-Vibeke Holst, "Du er fucking sexistisk, Niarn!," *Politiken*, November 13, 2004. All translations from Danish are are mine.

65 Charlotte Jørgensen, "Debattens væsen og uvæsen. Om fjendtlighed i den offentlige debat," *Retorik Studier* 10 (1995), 8. My translation.

66 Ibid., 30.

In this respect, I caution that a reading considering only the two primary texts by Hanne-Vibeke Holst and Niarn renders too simple a picture. Several participants engaged in the debate about public language and the construction of gender, some of whom were women with an insider's knowledge of hip hop culture.[67] In addition, the debate was probably initiated well before Holst's intervention, perhaps in the previous year (2003) in the Danish newspaper *Berlingske Tidende*, which ran a feature following a British media storm, or even earlier, when *Den Gale Pose* made its first appearance in 1995.[68] Likewise, it is hard to establish an exact time for its ending; as late as 2005, the hip hop singer Jokeren commented on the debate in a rap lyric which in turn resulted in new coverage in the newspapers.

My primary objects of analysis, however, are the texts by Holst and Niarn, while the song "Mit Sprog YO" (2005) by Jokeren, another Danish hip hop artist, is included for perspective. What follows is the first paragraph of Holst's letter:

> Dear Niarn!
> Congratulations on the reception of your new album "Year 79" [Årgang 79]. I am year 59, myself, and like you, from the North of Jutland, so if the dice had been thrown differently, I could almost have been your worried Mum up there, while you were fucking around like a semi-criminal badazz. However, I'm too old to have been "that bitch who left you in Aalborg," and, generally, you probably think I'm too outdated to pay any attention to. Actually, I admit, I don't fancy listening to a gangsta rapper like yourself, and other screwed up hip hop boys. And if I didn't have both a teenage daughter and a teenage son, I would hardly have bothered to get excited. Then maybe, I wouldn't have noticed how somebody like you pol-

67 Rune Skyum-Nielsen, *Nr. 1. Dansk hiphopkultur siden 1983* (København: Informations forlag, 2006), 142.

68 Ibid.,142.

> lutes what we grown-ups call "the public sphere." To stick to your own terminology, you let so much fucking sexist and violence-glorifying shit out that one has to soundproof oneself not to get soiled. And any normal young person, who can't do a school physics assignment without the company of MTV, Boogie, or P3, doesn't.[69]

Immediately, we understand that Holst is parodying the style of gangsta rap, and that she argues to some extent by way of disdain for the rapper Niarn and his art. The parody is found concretely in Holst's imitation of some elements of style from the hip hop universe. These are, among others, certain expressions of slang (for instance, "badazz"), frequent use of sexual and scatological metaphors (for instance, "let so much fucking sexist and violence-glorifying shit out"), and certain themes concerning identity based on gender, language, generation, or locality.

After this introductory paragraph, Holst tones down the parody and confirms her speaking persona, established above, as the mother of two teenage children. This is done by posing a number of rhetorical questions that are all based on a topos of influence – the influence of bad language and its long term effects on society.

Holst ties this to a suggestion that Niarn take responsibility for his language and the attitudes he expresses. By the end, she returns to the environmental metaphor already established in the first paragraph:

> Dear Niarn, it's cool enough that you can turn the power of the north into the power of words. But then you should also realize that words do not just disappear into the atmosphere. Words do not just become earth, but may ooze down and poison the groundwater of our common mind. That applies not least to *bitch, whore, slut*. Sooner or later, you will also have

69 Hanne-Vibeke Holst, "Du er fucking sexistisk, Niarn!"

> to take responsibility. At any rate, so far it has been Danish environmental politics that the polluter pays.[70]

Evidently, the environmental metaphor has an argumentative function, and is an apt example of Fahnestock's general claim that rhetorical figures are condensed arguments. The metaphor works like a condensed argument, and as it is developed and nuanced throughout the text, it argues the case that Niarn's view on women will affect young people and their view on gender and sexuality. Consequently Niarn, who is an idol to teenagers, must take responsibility.

One explanation for Holst's decision to argue with rhetorical figures like metaphor and rhetorical questions could be that the analogy between language and environment stalls. In comparison to environmental contamination, the effect of 'pollution' through words is somewhat harder to verify. Thus, she is unable to simply assert that the lyrics of the rapper are damaging to young people, but makes her case by changing the 'burden of proof': "Can that be ruled out, Niarn? Can it be ruled out that your attitude and your tough lyrics incite young boys to cultivate a destructive macho-identity as sex-fixated city-warriors with one hand on the knife handle and the other down the panty? Can it?"[71]

In his rejoinder, Niarn basically acknowledges that he needs to explain himself. It has the headline: "I am Fucking Realistic, Hanne!," imitating her own headline with the rhetorical figure *paronomasia* by using a repetition with a minimal change, from "sexist" to "realistic".[72] In Fahnestock's terms, this would count as an example of how a rhe-

---

70 Ibid.

71 Ibid.

72 In fact, the rhetorical figure *paronomasia* is a repetition of one word, according to *Retorisk leksikon*, where Eide defines it as a kind of wordplay in which one word is repeated with a minimal change, resulting in a semantic 'jump.' Tormod Eide, *Retorisk leksikon* (Oslo: Spartacus forlag, 1999), 105. Above, I use the term more loosely.

torical figure establishes the idea iconically. Furthermore, the headline demonstrates that Niarn is a reflective language user, and that the debate is about language and art, and not just gender roles.

Holst constructed her speaker persona as an adult, and conversely, Niarn as a mischievous teenager who "pollutes what we grown-ups call 'the public sphere.'" This is not a role that Niarn accepts. On the contrary, the style in his letter is distinct from Holst's, and even more so from his own lyrics. It is reasoned and patiently argumentative, and the opinions he holds are moderate. He practises good debate ethics and is accommodating to Holst's arguments: "I fully understand your concern regarding your own children's safety, but [...]."[73] The letter meets the ideals of public debate in all particulars; in fact it almost looks like a subtle parody of the style used in "what we grown-ups call 'the public sphere.'" But it is probably not a parody, since Niarn uses this style to argue his case. He constructs his ethos as an adult and reasoned artist who has, moreover, seen through Holst's attempt to transform her ethos as a mother to rhetorical agency:

> Dear Hanne!
> Congratulations on your contribution to a debate in this newspaper, we can all use the publicity, whether we sell records or books. I shall not, arrogantly, attempt to deny that I am aware of who you are. Your name and especially your opinions came to my attention several times during my childhood. You and a lot of other self-appointed experts have made your contribution to shaping the world and the society that I have been brought up in – the very world and society that I depict in my lyrics. My album has the title "Year 79" because it is an exposition of my upbringing in a world with all the shades that we all know and fear. I have not created a world with

73 Niarn, "Jeg er fucking realistisk, Hanne!", *Politiken*, November 20 (2004). My translation.

drugs and violence – it is a world with drugs and violence that has created me.[74]

This last sentence contains a repetition of words in successive clauses with reversed grammatical order so that the semantic function of the 'I' creating the world is reversed for the world changing the 'I.' It is the rhetorical figure *antimetabole*, and I shall immediately reveal that it sums up the argumentation of the letter. Towards the end, following a discussion of language's dynamic nature concluding in a claim that terms like 'whore' should be understood in their context, Niarn returns to the reversed repetition in order to clarify his view on language and art: "The question is whether the artist creates new attitudes and tendencies with his art, or whether the art just reflects the society in which it is created."[75] This time it is not *antimetabole*, but the rhetorical figure *chiasmus*, where the reversal is semantic and does not involve a precise repetition of words. It may be viewed as a relaxed version of the *antimetabole*, as Fahnestock would have it, but in this case, the looser reversal has a more specific function in relation to Niarn's argument. It is simply an assertion that is less categorical – as it is also spelled out in his addition: "The truth probably lies somewhere in between, namely, that there is an interaction between society and art."[76]

The consideration of the argumentative function of rhetorical figures and style turns out to be useful in the critical analysis of Niarn's deliberation. The rhetorical figures function as textual and argumentative focal points that lead, analytically, into the kernel of the argumentation. One advantage to approaching argumentation from this angle is that the analysis is not aimed at testing the validity of arguments or evaluating them ethically; rather, it establishes a viewpoint for observing the dynamics and topics of argumentation. More precisely, it

74 Ibid.

75 Niarn, "Jeg er fucking realistisk, Hanne!"

76 Ibid.

proves to be a key to analyzing the conceptual power struggle among the debaters – that is, their battle to win the conceptual control to define and interpret the possible rhetorical effect and social impact of language. Additionally, it is evident that style and parody of style play a role in their argumentation and that this broader aspect cannot be accounted for by the analysis of rhetorical figures. Both debaters very consciously use style to argue by establishing ethos and agency, or conversely, by attacking the opponent's character and mandate to speak.

Finally, I shall make a rhetorical critical point on my choice of artifact. Whereas Fahnestock intended to show that rhetorical figures can be found in scientific discourse as in every other discourse, my analysis confirms that style and rhetorical figures apply to public debate, a central field of rhetorical criticism. This, of course, does not preclude a consideration of works of art. In a remark in the same debate, the Danish rapper Jokeren at least claims that rap is an argumentative genre. Contrary to Niarn, who had to perform a style of reason and responsibility in participating in the 'real' public debate, Jokeren deliberates in a song lyric:

> Focus on one word and preclude the rest?
> Is that what you call a debate?
> Or do you just rip off Danish bastard rap?
> Because I choose to say what I mean?
> What you call "sexism", I call "rhetoric".[77]

Here, Jokeren reprises both Holst's headline "You are Fucking Sexist, Niarn!" and Niarn's wordplay and *paronomasia* in his headline "I am Fucking Realistic, Hanne!" The replacement of the central words marks a change in topos which enables Niarn to turn it into a debate about art rather than gender politics. In this respect, Jokeren's com-

---

77 Jokeren, *Gigolo Jesus* (2005).

ment is significant because he clearly addresses Holst and changes the topos to "rhetoric." With an allusion to the previous debate, he asserts he is "fucking rhetorical," that is, using language and style strategically and purposefully. According to Jokeren's line of argument, the obvious existence of sexist language is not the objective of hip hop; it is a feature among others in a highly codified hip hop style. Along with hand signs and demonstrations of skills in rhyme and rhythm, the slang, the boasting, and the 'dissing' perform a rhetorical style strategically aimed at shaping the rapper's identity and rhetorical agency.[78]

78 Pedersen, Birgitte Stougaard, "Go stil dér!," *Rhetorica Scandinavica* 52 (2009), 38.

CHAPTER THREE

STYLE AND THE POSTMODERN

In the introduction to an article on style in *Ästhetische Grundbegriffe* (2003), the German literary theorist Rainer Rosenberg sums up the relationship between style and twentieth-century arts and aesthetics as paradoxical: As style became a key issue in academic aesthetic disciplines – notably in the historiography of art – it lost its influence in the arts. Or, to be more precise, Rosenberg observes that the scholarly interest in style as a collective phenomenon – a concrete form that reflects the spirit or ideas of an epoch – flourished at a time when style ceased to be a collective phenomenon in the arts. As an academic concept in the aesthetic disciplines, style was valued as a form that could reflect the content and creative processes of pre-modern art. In this respect, Rosenberg concludes, the lack of a category of style in some postmodern theories corresponds with their perception that style no longer has a cognitive potential in contemporary art.[1]

Rosenberg's description is arguably accurate; much of the value of the style concept in aesthetic theories consisted in its alleged ability to capture the spirit (of an artist, a work of art, an epoch, or a nation). According to Wolfgang G. Müller's theory, discussed in chapter one, the nineteenth-century aesthetic disciplines were to a great extent

1 Rainer Rosenberg, "Stil: Einleitung," in *Ästhetische Grundbegriffe*, vol. 5, ed. K. Barck et al. (Stuttgart: Metzler, 2003), 648.

dominated by a perception of style as a coherence of form and content – found in the topoi of style as man, style as idea, or style as nation. Therefore, as contemporary art and literature came to defy this representational experience, style stopped being of value as a critical concept.

Aspects of style did not, however, cease to be of importance in aesthetic disciplines. Along with a general interest in formalistic aspects in aesthetic studies in the late twentieth century, a linguistic or rhetorical 'turn' in the literary studies of this time is well-documented. Structuralist and poststructuralist literary theories were preoccupied with conceptual questions that had traditionally been central to rhetorical theories, and some of them shared a marked interest in rhetorical figures. Theories of a poststructuralist bent especially found in the elocutionary elements a source for a metaphysical critique reminiscent of sophistic rhetoric.

From a rhetorical perspective, however, these literary theories are not 'rhetorical' in any traditional or historical sense of rhetoric. A telling example of the displacement of rhetorical style can be found in the writings of the literary deconstructivist Paul de Man, who sometimes referred to his critical enterprise as 'rhetoric', when a more precise naming for his analytic scrutiny of certain rhetorical tropes and figures would be 'deconstruction'. Although a simple identification of rhetoric and deconstruction is unwarranted, some of the insights produced in the wake of the textualist and deconstructive paradigm have been adapted by rhetorical theory. Of particular note is the metaphysical critique of transcendent subjects and meaning, performed in a variety of disciplines under such labels as deconstruction, postmodernism, poststructuralism, discourse analysis, and postcolonialism, recognizable as the epistemological premise of constitutive rhetoric that I discussed in chapter one.

The present chapter is devoted to the development of style in recent rhetorical criticism. In chapter two, we witnessed how the study of rhetorical figures and metaphor caused twentieth-century theories to reflect on the traditional elocutionary topos and revise it, mostly on the basis of a theory of constitutive rhetoric. However, slightly differing traditions of thinking about style have been evoked during the last twenty to thirty years. These studies have proclaimed an interest in a concept of style which relates to aesthetics, sensibility, emotions, and taste. It is a concept of style which includes – but cannot be reduced to – *elocutio* and rhetorical figures. The present rhetorical revival of style is thus shaped by a thinking of style in terms of aesthetic sensibility and taste which has formerly been a hallmark of aesthetic studies – paradoxically at a time when aesthetic studies have, in turn, abandoned the style concept almost completely.

Before I commence this inquiry, I feel I should be explicit about my approach to the somewhat toxic cocktail of postmodern theories, rhetoric, and style. It is my intention neither to diminish nor deny the influence of postmodern thought on some theories of rhetoric or style (or vice versa). However, I do mean to caution that the discussions be exercised with conceptual precision, which is the only way to avoid the unfortunate largeness and looseness of 'rhetoric' and 'style' that have often been the confusing center of attention in studies that relate postmodern thinking and rhetorical style.

One example of this tendency will suffice: In the same way that rhetoric and its many traditions cannot be identified with deconstruction, style resists a reduction to 'mere form'. In an attempt to write a history of style, the German literary critic Hans Ulrich Gumbrecht finds in deconstruction a concept of style which is compatible with the oldest in our culture. Notably, Gumbrecht detects a fascination with the materiality of writing in the American literary critic Geoffrey Hartman's reading of Derrida's *Glas*:

> Die Schrift als Spur, das Einritzen, das Loschen der Spur. Diesen Stil, diese Schrift ('écriture') rückt Hartman in ein 'systematische Position,' die dem philosophischen Status der monolithischen Begriffe von 'Wirklichkeit' und 'Wahrheit' vergleichbar ist. Stil und Schrift sind für ihn das Eigentliche, gegenüber dem Begriffe wie 'Subjekt,' 'Bewuβtsein' oder

> 'Wahrheit' zu schieren Effekten verblassen, so wie man seit Plato immer wieder Sprache und Stil als 'bloβen Schmuck,' als 'Mittel zum Zweck der Wahrheit' abgewertet hatte.[2]

As I have already argued, the interest that *some* postmodern theories have had in *some aspects* of style does not allow for such a firm conjunction of postmodernism and style. In chapter one, I have leaned on the more specific terms of 'constitutive rhetoric' and 'constitutive style' to describe a rhetoric and a style marked by postmodernism. Although some common ground of constitutive style and poststructuralism is evident, the reduction of style to *écriture* evinces a lack of historical and conceptual sensitivity.

Furthermore, and perhaps symptomatic of Gumbrecht's literary frame of reference, his history of style associates it with writing as opposed to speech. This distinction he traces to the Roman playwright Terence, who in the second century BC opposed *stilus* to *oratio*; and in Gumbrecht's history of style, this provides the basis for a displacement of the meaning of style as "die schriftliche Performanz" and *oratio* as "mündliche Performanz."[3] According to Gumbrecht, this line of argument is compatible with Niklas Luhmann's proposal that the modern history of the style concept is related to the institutionalization of the printed book. As I have explained above, such reductions are, however, unwarranted in the history of style.[4]

---

2 Hans Ulrich Gumbrecht, "Schwindende Stabilität der Wirklichkeit. Eine Geschichte des Stilbegriffs", in H. U. Gumbrecht & K. L. Pfeiffer, eds., *Stil. Geschichten und Funktionen eines kulturwissenschaftlichen Diskurselements* (Frankfurt am Main: Suhrkamp Taschenbuch Verlag, 1986), 780.

3 Ibid., 730.

4 Similar attempts to dichotomize style as writing versus rhetoric as spoken language have also been rejected by Ulla Fix, Andreas Gardt, and Joachim Knape: "Neither is the occasional limitation of rhetoric to spoken language and the reduction of stylistics to writing legitimate. Although it got its start in predominantly oral culture, rhetoric has been applied to written texts since the middle ages. Stylis-

Styles of Power and Politics

If not to clear, then at least to tidy the ground for an examination of style in recent rhetorical criticism, I have sought to bracket the concept of rhetorical style from some of the more common assumptions about poststructuralism. In order to do so, I have introduced the concept of constitutive rhetorical style, which is a postmodern interpretation of style founded in rhetorical traditions. This concept is part of a rhetorical paradigm where *rhetoric is thought of as social action*, and *style is regarded to be constitutive of identity, argumentation, and rhetorical norms.*

In *Political Style. The Artistry of Power* (1995), the American rhetorical critic Robert Hariman does not confine his concept of style to language or individual style, but includes a variety of actions and symbolic choices, such as gesture, décor, ornament, and the absence of speech, in his analysis of the norms of a political culture. To him, the ability to read and perform style is guided by an aesthetic sensibility of taste, manners, charisma, and decorum, and his study aims to turn an experience of how some political encounters depend on style into a method for analyzing and criticizing how style works as a rhetorical strategy within specific relations of power.

Political style, to Hariman, is "a coherent repertoire of rhetorical conventions depending on aesthetic reactions for political effect", a definition which stresses how political style operates as *a rhetoric*, that is, a catalog of the means of persuasion characteristic of a particular political culture.[5] The outcome is practical and strategic, as the knowledge of the ways and workings of a style equips the reader to act skillfully within a characteristic situation, and critical, as analysis and criticism of particular styles adds to an understanding of some aspects of our social reality which are commonly considered inexplicable or irrational.

---

tics, on the other hand, has also been oriented around speech at least since the development of modern discourse analysis." Ulla Fix et al., "Introduction", xii.

5 Robert Hariman, *Political Style. The Artistry of Power* (Chicago: The University of Chicago Press, 1995), 4.

Hariman's own study identifies four specific political styles: the courtly, realist, bureaucratic, and republican. The courtly style, which is designed to demonstrate the power of sovereigns, is characterized by a displacement of speech and communication with bodily gestures and immobility. Although Hariman reassures his reader that the courtly style has little political significance in the democratic institutions of today, he concedes that certain traces can be found in mass media representations of political events. Whereas the courtly style is largely pre-modern, the realist style constitutes an essentially modern world. It works by an assertive separation of power and textuality as it situates power in the pragmatic realm of nature, common sense, practical ability and result – and in complete contempt and negligence of the more speculative enterprises of ethics and arts. From a rhetorical perspective, however, the graver implication of the realist style seems to be that it so obviously adjures deliberation.

The same can be said about the second example of a style suited to the modern world, the bureaucratic style, which subordinates activity, spontaneity, and initiative in political actors to routine and rigor. Writing is the preferred communicative modus in the bureaucratic style, which finds its paradigm practice in office culture where hierarchy, endless case handling, and official ethos are valued highly. The last of Hariman's studies deals with the republican style, the only one of the four that Hariman actually recommends, although his analysis of Cicero's letters to Atticus also reveals its deficiencies. In this particular political style, oratorical virtuosity is valued for its public performance in a parliamentary culture. It includes appreciation of verbal skill, and it guards certain norms that are shared within a rhetorical culture, especially norms of consensus, civic virtue, and disinterested vestments. However, its elements of excessive subjectivity, performance, and drama, which commingle the private self with the public agenda, seem – viewed through the modern lenses of political science and social theory – of less value.

His own project Hariman deems "cautious postmodernism."[6] He neither identifies with some postmodern notions that all thought and action are stylized, nor does he believe that style is mere ornament or purely manipulative. Nevertheless, he argues that modern societies have become defenseless against aesthetic manipulation, because of a separation of politics and aesthetics as autonomous realms of experience in the early modern period. As a result, objectivity has been made the standard in politics and science, whereas the deliberative practices of aesthetics and arts are thought of as merely subjective. In an attempt to disrupt this order, Hariman's study of political style aims for an increased understanding of how aesthetic dimensions shape and influence particular political cultures.

Much of Hariman's discussion of style and politics thrives on a rather stern dichotomy between art and rhetoric, a separation which has its roots in Romantic and modern conceptions of art and aesthetics. From this perspective, style belongs to the autonomously aesthetic realm, and within this framework, Hariman's study is a rehabilitation of an understanding of a rhetorical style which is not bereft of associations with the pragmatic and the political. As the study is arguably aimed at a community of rhetorical critics, its positioning of style as art and diametrically opposed to politics seems a shade forced.

In addition, Hariman does not situate style within a general theoretical or ethical paradigm. Style is an aesthetic aspect of rhetoric, a pragmatic choice as well as an analytical category, yet in some respects, it remains essentially instrumental. Or, as Bradford Vivian notes in his critique of Hariman's cautious postmodernism: "Rather than questioning the classical, predominantly rational, ethos of autonomous rhetorical action, this definition neutralizes the aesthetic and affective capacities of style by regarding it merely as one available means of persuasion, thereby reducing rhetoric to the individual

6 Hariman, *Political Style*, 6.

mastery of persuasive conventions, to skill in matters of 'decorum.'"[7] Although Vivian acknowledges that Hariman's style concept is situated within a political culture, he regrets that "rhetoric and style in Hariman's account remain essentially rational, purposeful communicative resources."[8] According to Vivian, this limits "the radical interpretive possibilities raised by Hariman's recognition of style as an organizing feature of social and political relations."[9]

My own regret is that Hariman does not account for style in relation to its basic semiotics. To mention a few pertinent questions generated from the topics of style: Is political style something you add to political substance when aiming for a specific effect? Or is it the essential expression of values and ideology in a political culture? Or, rather, does a political style constitute the policy as it is performed and rehearsed? Although these are some of the questions that have preoccupied scholars from Antiquity to today, they are not explicitly addressed by Hariman.

The Style of Postmodern Culture

Much more explicit is the discussion of the semiotics of style in Bradford Vivian's "Style, Rhetoric, and Postmodern Culture" (2002). In this article, he unpacks the claim of the French sociologist Michel Maffesoli that style is the crystallizing sentiment of the postmodern epoch. In a treatise on style, Maffesoli has argued that the modernist social and political ideals of reason, production, and order cannot account for the nature of postmodern society and politics.[10] In present-day societies we witness how individuals form opinions according to shared beliefs and

7 Bradford Vivian, "Style, Rhetoric, and Postmodern Culture," *Philosophy and Rhetoric* 35, 3 (2002), 225.

8 Ibid.

9 Ibid.

10 Ibid., 226. Michel Maffesoli, *The Contemplation of the World: Figures of Community Style* (Minneapolis: University of Minnesota Press, 1996).

values about, for instance, religion, ethnicity, territory, or linguistics. Maffesoli refers to the growing importance of such phenomena as postmodern tribalism. This tribalism is sustained in irrational celebrations that are driven by a sense of the superfluous and a search for the qualitative. Instead of gazing towards a realization of an ideal society in a distant future, the new culture values a "being-togetherness" in the present. However, traditional values are not simply opposed or supplanted by tribal social practices. Rather, the relationship between the two takes the form of a subtle metamorphosis of values, resulting in a new configuration.[11] That reconfiguration may best be described in terms of style:

> Rather than a consensual agenda or utilitarian rationale, the emerging animus of society is most evocatively described as a sentiment, passion, or collective effervescence. In a word, the current epoch appears to be informed, at least in its nascent stages, by an unprecedented investment in the *aesthetic*. Most notably, the present ubiquity of public spectacle has become a sustaining element of diverse social pursuits, from consumer culture and civic elements to humanitarian causes and political programs. At such a historical moment, the category of *style* offers renewed explanatory force.[12]

Style, in Maffesoli's understanding, is the distinctive expression of a cultural moment: At first sight this appears to be a fairly traditional account of epochal or period style. But a closer look reveals that Maffesoli's concept of period style is neither structured according

11 Maffesoli's text offers a more elaborate account: "The different constitutive elements of modernity are not 'superseded,' in the dialectical sense of the term; nor are they finished, as it is too often the custom to say. In, fact, one cannot deny that they continue to play a role in social life, but imperceptibly they take on another timbre, and their tonality is no longer the same." Ibid., 21-22.

12 Vivian, "Style, Rhetoric, and Postmodern Culture," 228.

to the nineteenth-century topoi of style as man or style as period, nor captured by the description of style as the essential sentiment of an epoch. Rather, Vivian stresses that Maffesoli understands style as constitutive: "For Maffesoli, style does not refer to an antiquated distinction between form and substance, but to the manner in which the representative aesthetic forms of a cultural epoch constitute its defining and substantive features."[13]

Maffesoli views the current, postmodern period as a culture of sentiment, and it is because of this general aesthetization of life that style is warranted to account for the growing influence on contemporary social relationships.[14] Following Maffesoli's analysis of the decreased interest in the public sphere in postmodern culture, Vivian argues that the concept of style offers a new evaluative frame. Whereas traditional democratic ideals are ill equipped to recognize how the political is no longer confined to civic forums, the concept of style is sensitive to the nature of postmodern society and politics, especially 'communitarian' values which are based on common emotions and sentiments rather than social contracts.[15] According to Vivian, a 'rhetoric of collective style' is aesthetic and affective, rather than conceptual and rational: "By this logic, we 'touch' one another rhetorically – that is, we communicate affectively in the service of some pragmatic collective purpose – through sentiment, aesthetic, or performance, instead of reason, ideals, or consensus."[16]

Maffesoli's identification of an emerging communitarian ideal underscores the changed understanding of the social character of the individual: "In a postmodern *épistémé*, the self is not so much an autonomous agent who exists prior to the influence of social and political relations as it is an embodiment of certain capacities for agency

13 Ibid.

14 Ibid., 228.

15 Ibid., 230-231.

16 Ibid., 238.

formed at their intersection."[17] This, in fact, encapsulates what Vivian believes to be Maffesoli's truly radical insight: that the individual is not an isolated atom, but exists in and is shaped by a particular social milieu.

According to Vivian, the modernist ideal of an autonomous individual has lost its former ethos in a cultural epoch shaped by unprecedented social heterogeneity and interdependence: "The widespread contemporary experience of such heterogeneity and interdependence cannot be explained by principles of reason, utility, or citizenship, but by the function of a collective aesthetic, a shared sentiment."[18] It follows that in a postmodern society where the self is a product of the changing needs and desires of the community, "the expression and maintenance of different social identities, the ethical practices that make possible particular forms of subjectivity, have emerged as the defining political investments of the postmodern era."[19]

Vivian's own contribution to the study of style and postmodern culture is his suggestion that a rhetorical inquiry can address the nature of aesthetic dissemination in a particular style: Not only can a rhetorical inquiry "account for the discursive means (the specific tropes, symbols, and rituals) by which a given style is engendered, maintained, or transfigured," it may also be used to "evaluate the affective or aesthetic practices according to which a particular collective sentiment establishes communication between cultural groups."[20]

Style as the Construction of Identity

The reduction of style to the intentions or actions of an individual agent is one of the main targets of Vivian's critical argument, but he does not specifically deny it, either. He concludes: "I do not mean

17 Ibid, 235.

18 Ibid, 236.

19 Ibid.

20 Ibid., 239.

to suggest that something called individual rhetorical agency does not exist; instead, I argue that such agency is fundamentally shaped by existing discursive and aesthetic conditions, which vary from one social context to another."[21]

A similar answer to the question of intentionality and style is given by Barry Brummett in *A Rhetoric of Style* (2008). According to Brummett, style is not so much something that one does; rather, it is the grounds upon which something is done. Like Vivian, Brummett is not above employing style for desired ends, but the strategic aspect of style has, by comparison, greater impact on Brummet's study. Rhetoric he defines as communication that influences others, and style is what we use when we "make claims about ourselves and others in order to bring about desired results."[22] More akin to lifestyle and popular culture than perhaps to traditional rhetoric, style is, in Brummett's definition:

> a complex system of actions, objects, and behaviors that is used to form messages that announce who we are, who we want to be, and who we want to be considered akin to. It is therefore also a system of communication with rhetorical influence on others. And as such, style is a means by which power and advantage are negotiated, distributed, and struggled over in society.[23]

Brummett's constructivist conception is derived from a binary distinction between two models of stylistic meaning. In the first model, style is communicative in a conventional sense: One picks elements of style that communicate a reality about the self, about how one is in fact. In the other 'semiotic model,' which to Brummett appears

---

21 Ibid., 241.

22 Barry Brummett, *A Rhetoric of Style* (Carbondale: Southern Illinois University Press, 2008), xi.

23 Ibid.

the stronger, it is held that who or what one is develops as a result of the style one displays. To illustrate this, in the first model one is cool and chooses certain styles to express that, whereas, in the second, one is cool because one displays certain styles.[24] If we compare Brummett's categories with the topoi on which my study is founded, the traditional model is identical with Müller's Romantic of topos style as man, whereas Brummett's semiotic model is the equivalent of the topos of style as constitutive.

Touching upon the complaint that style is mere surface, Brummett like most rhetorical critics claims that style is substance. Yet his explanation is not like that of most rhetoricians. Drawing on a host of authorships that may casually be grouped as postmodern – Judith Butler, Jean Baudrillard, Jacques Lacan, and Zygmunt Bauman, to mention at least some of the names on Brummett's extensive list of sources – his argument goes like this: "If we live in a culture that is increasingly one of sign and image, then a style made of sign and image may be as 'real' as it gets, as real as anybody wants or needs for it to be."[25]

However, Brummett maintains that signs never float completely. The semiotics of style works by retaining some meaning from original referents, but it is a meaning that it is no longer closely connected to. From his ample pool of examples, here is one about the style performed by wearing a cowboy hat:

> The sign that is a cowboy hat, for instance, need not be "anchored" to any real cowboy, nor would one nowadays assume that someone wearing a cowboy hat has that occupation. The concept of floating signs is quite widespread and is useful but cannot be absolutely true, for signs never float completely. For a cowboy hat to have a meaning at all – for it to retain the

24 Ibid., 35.

25 Ibid., 10-11.

meanings of rugged, rural individualism that allow it to work within certain systems of style – it has to retain some tether of meaning, however long and stretched, to the original cowboys who first wore them.[26]

The semiotic operation of appropriating signs from the contexts that originally gave them meaning is essential to style. Brummett borrows the term "bricolage" from a study of subculture and style among (notably) British punks by Dick Hebdige, who in turn borrowed it from Levi-Strauss' anthropological analysis of the function of magical modes. Hebdige observes how, in punk style, the shifting of signs and their meanings from one context to another works: "Objects borrowed from the most sordid of contexts found a place in the punk's ensembles: lavatory chains were draped in graceful arcs across chests encased in plastic bin-liners. Safety pins were taken out of their domestic 'utility' context and worn as gruesome ornaments through the cheek, ear or lip."[27]

Similarly, Brummett borrows the term "homology" from Hebdige and Levi-Strauss, which is "the symbolic fit between the values and the lives of a group."[28] Even a seemingly chaotic subculture like punk is held together by a thoroughly ordered system of coherence. Indeed, outside the realm of subculture, homology shapes the performance and analysis of particular styles, such as Bauhaus, Romantic, or working-class, by establishing cohesive clusters that work as unified sign systems, holding together sets of signs, actions, images, objects, movements, gestures, and vocabularies.[29]

---

26 Ibid., 8.

27 Dick Hebdige, *Subculture. The Meaning of Style* (Taylor & Francis e-Library, [1979] 2002), 107.

28 Ibid., 113.

29 Maffesoli's conception of style operates on a similar principle of unity which Vivian finds unfortunate because of certain "Hegelian overtones." However, Maffesoli elsewhere accentuates the heterogeneity of style: "Whatever 'unity' Maffesoli as-

Outside the immediate interest of this study, Brummett also purports a view of style as a global semiotic system, "one rhetoric," which is maintained though the media. Acknowledging some variations of, for instance, culture, class, and race that call for rhetorical specialization and sensitivity, Brummett imagines style as a social system that embraces "an increasingly global terrain of shared knowledge, action, and judgment."[30] The idea of a unified cultural system in late capitalism is grounded in numerous statements about our postmodern world, such as: "Late-capitalist societies are more and more preoccupied with style."[31] Brummett's argumentation here resonates with some of the points made by Vivian and Maffesoli, but while their observations are tied to a comprehensive analysis of the deliberative practices of our present society, Brummett's claims are supported by fiercely analytical scrutiny of everyday practice. By comparison, Brummett's implied celebration of the postmodern condition and the aesthetization of everyday life is slightly more distinct: "Style is a cultural preoccupation with signs and images, grounded in aesthetics. Such a preoccupation flourishes under conditions usually described as postmodern, conditions of decenteredness, flux, polysemy, flow."[32]

---

cribes to the style of an epoch must be taken in its most metaphorical sense: style, he explains, 'is the postmodern form of the social link – a social link "in dotted outline," shaken by violent, chaotic, and unforeseen jolts.'" Maffesoli, "Treatise on Style," 34. Vivian, "Style, Rhetoric, and Postmodern Culture," 229.

30 Brummett, *A Rhetoric of Style*, xiii.

31 Ibid., 17.

32 Ibid., 32. Vivian discusses at length what he deems to be an unfortunate flirtation with the transformed political values on the part of Maffesoli: "Even if a 'being-togetherness' currently reigns, there are factions whose shared passion, for a variety of reasons, one would not want to be shared; from Western militia and white supremacist groups to religious fundamentalists throughout the world, shared hatreds rather than coherent political visions unite a broad spectrum of individuals around a common purpose." Vivian, "Style, Rhetoric, and Postmodern Culture," 232.

Some of the premises of Maffesoli and Brummett will not be pursued in the present study. Most importantly, I shall not discuss further their shared assumption that late-modern societies and their political cultures are preoccupied with aesthetics, spectacle, and style. This idea is closely intertwined with the historical assertion that postmodern society is "increasingly" or "more and more" influenced by aesthetics, predominant in Brummett's argument as well as in Maffesoli's idea that style is the crystallizing sentiment of the current epoch.[33] These assumptions about style, contemporary society and politics, and, more implicitly, the past, I understand to be grounded in primarily sociological disciplines and methodologies. My own exploration of rhetorical style is conceptual and interprets style in relation to postmodern theories, rather than postmodern societies. I contribute to an analysis of contemporary society only in so far as my investigation partakes in criticism of rhetorical action and deliberative practices. Like Brummett and Vivian, I see style as constitutive, but my study is founded on a thesis about the importance of rhetorical style in political communication, not on a claim about the predomination of style in postmodern culture. In particular, the implied historical claim that style has played a minor role in centuries past seems to be out of step with the rhetorical tradition.

Constituting Political and Social Identity

The political aspects of style's role in an aesthetisized postmodern culture can be traced in the construction of the social identity of

33 Contrarily, a skeptical view on the implied historical claim is indicated by Vivian: "The majority of the rhetorical tradition demonstrates (although Hariman's account suggests modern rhetoricians have lost sight of the fact) that the practical exercise of politics seldom has been conducted without attention to ceremony, performances, and popular taste; even a cultural aversion to sentiment is still a kind of cultural sentiment." Ibid.

individuals or groups. To Brummett – as to Vivian and Maffesoli – style actively shapes identity politics, especially in organizing the social. Following Althusser's idea of how texts "interpellate" people to adopt certain subject positions, discussed in chapter one in terms of constitutive rhetoric, Brummett observes how style functions in the same way, calling people to become certain subjects and to organize themselves in certain ways. In effect, style operates through the taste and aesthetic judgment of individuals who get to know themselves as groups through the different aesthetics that mark their styles. Although Brummett's argument subscribes to a theory of constitutive rhetoric, the idea somewhat resembles Edwin Black's more limited proposition that stylistic tokens in discourse function as marks of identification for the audience, as they form a "second persona," that is, a model of who the speaker would have the auditor become.[34]

Below, I cite one of Brummett's particularly powerful examples of a political organization established through collective, constitutive style:

> In 1822, the recently crowned King of Great Britain, George IV, visited Scotland, the first monarch to do so since 1641. Questions of Scottish political and social identity were in the balance. It had not been too many years since Prince Charles Stewart in 1745 led the last serious armed attempt to put a Scottish king on the throne of England or failing that to recover Scottish independence. Increasing economic and social ties were weakening the insularity of traditional Scottish society, however. Scots were weighing issues of who they were and what was their relationship to the British people to the south. George IV's own dynasty began not too many years before with the German George I, who spoke no English whatsoever.

34 Black, "The Second Persona," 334.

George IV had to be received in just the right way to juggle all these sensitive political balls successfully.

To solve the problem, that grand old man of Scotland, Sir Walter Scott, gave a party. Scott was "hugely popular," "a major international force" – and author of the romantic *Waverly*, "one of the most significant book of the nineteenth century."[35] Scott was in some ways as much a man of our time as his. He understood the power of style, surface, and floating signs. Scott is widely regarded as the inventor of the historical novel, spinning compelling tales of knights in armor and Gothic dungeons that neither his public nor he had ever seen. We might regard him as a preelectronic expert in the art of creating hugely successful simulations for the public. His party for the king was to be an exercise of that talent.

Scott gathered the heads of the "clans" of Scotland, a kind of social organization that had been fading in importance for some time as modernism crept north of the Tweed and the Clyde. Scott instructed these worthies to make kilts and matching regalia from the tartans of plaid cloths distinctive of each clan, and to wear them to the party for the King. The trouble was, Scott was told, many clans had no such thing as a tartan. Kilts, yes, but distinctive plaid designs designating their clans, no. Never you mind, said Scott, make something up. So the clan leaders did, dreaming up tartan patterns as if they had been hanging in the wardrobes of stone castles forever. As one historical source observes, "He practically re-invented Highland society and clan tartans (which had not previously

---

35 Brummett, *A Rhetoric of Style*, 74-75. "Writing Scotland, a Journey through Scotland's Literature: Walter Scott." *BBC*. July 1, 2006. http://www.bbc.co.uk/scotland/arts/writingscotland/learning_journeys/tartan_myths/walter_scott/.

existed in this form) for the visit."[36] Scott did so for the King as well, creating the "Royal Stewart" tartan design out of whole cloth, so to speak, a "false tartanry" that never existed before the party.[37] At any rate, George was a Hanover, not a Stewart. Scott even put the unfortunate monarch into a set of "salmon-pink leggings" to go with this Highland simulational outfit.[38] Although "heavily criticized" by some of his fellow Scots for this charade,[39] Scott's exercise in sartorial rhetoric was an instant popular success. The peaty aroma of ancient age attached to the tartans as if it had been around for centuries. Not only did the invented link between clan and tartan become a reality from that moment on but also the political challenges of cementing ties between the north and the British monarch were successfully addressed through that ploy. To this day, Scots wear tartans for special events, British monarchs reinscribe the invented tradition by wearing tartans on appropriate occasions, and Scotland shows no signs of outright secession or Jacobite rebellion.[40]

Evidently, the sartorial rhetoric amounted to more than a "bricolage," a transfer of signs and symbols from one context to another where they obtain new meanings. Rather, because tartan designs specific to each clan did not exist before, but had to be made up especially for the party, it is an illustrative example of created rhetorical style.

---

36 Brummett, *A Rhetoric of Style*, 74-75. "Famous Scotts: Sir Walter Schott (1771-1832)." July 1, 2006. http://www.rampantscotland.com/famous/blfamscott.htm.

37 Ibid.

38 Brummett, *A Rhetoric of Style*, 74-75. "Writing Scotland."

39 Ibid.

40 Brummett, *A Rhetoric of Style*, 74-75. Brummett's interpretation of an absence of secession in contemporary Scottish society has been overtaken by recent political currents. Note how the example contradicts the author's idea that style should be a singular characteristic of late-modern capitalist society.

Its re-invention of highland society and re-inscription of the king as a member of a unique culture makes it such a powerful instance of successful constitutive style that it might serve as a model for the constitution of national and political style more generally.

The remainder of this chapter is an investigation into the rhetorical constitution of national identity in a contemporary democracy – and specifically, it is devoted to an analysis of rhetorical style in a former Danish Prime Minister's rhetoric. Her political, styled communication occurs in various settings, but the main analytical artifact is an official speech from October 2011: the annual address given by the Prime Minister at the opening of the Danish Parliament, Folketinget. Compared to Brummett's study of the unorthodox Scottish solution, the political rhetoric of my inquiry is somewhat more conventional. Yet many of the aims and purposes are the same, specifically, the production of a collective style that is aimed at creating a shared sense of national identity.

Values and Words on the Danish Political Scene

Not only was it the first official speech that the newly elected Danish Prime Minster had to deliver, it was also the first Opening Address given by a social democrat in more than a decade – and the first ever by a woman. Prime Minister Helle Thorning-Schmidt had been the leader of the Danish Social Democratic Party since 2005. In her election speech to the party congress, she infamously boasted "Jeg kan slå Anders Fogh" ("I can beat Anders Fogh"), a catchy slogan deploying assonance as well as rhythm on the words "slå" (beat) and "Fogh" (the Prime Minister in power). It was also a cocky slogan which inevitably backfired when she did not put Anders Fogh Rasmussen out of office in the election in 2007.

In her time as leader, style had always been an issue. She was a slim, blonde, and beautiful woman who dressed elegantly in brigh- colored suits and high heels. One of her party colleagues even gave her the nickname "Gucci-Helle." Undisputedly, her impeccable looks were at odds with the traditional working-class image of the Social Democratic Party. But as a candidate dressed for political and national leadership, her rhetorical style seemed to promise a kairotic grasp of power: She looked like a Prime Minister long before she was one. Furthermore, Thorning-Schmidt's style did not have the appearance of political spin. No one would suspect that her beauty and class were the result of a makeover of a political geek. On the contrary, it all seemed natural to her. Her style seemed truly to be embedded in her personality; she was cool, elegant, and fit for the fight.

Physical appearance aside, the Opening Address is given by the leader of the Danish nation, and – among other characteristics that I shall return to – it is a rhetorical display of governance and leadership. In 2011, the victory of the Social Democratic Party was marginal, and Helle Thorning-Schmidt had – again – reduced the mandate by one. The social democrats formed a government with two other parties that were on different sides of the political spectrum, Det Radikale Venstre leaning to the right, and a party further to the left, Socialistisk Folkeparti.

The former Danish government, a tight alliance between the liberalist Venstre and the Conservative Party supported by a third, nationalist party, Dansk Folkeparti, had been in power for ten years. The first and most prominent Prime Minister in this period, Anders Fogh Rasmussen, had in 2001 introduced values that the government had maintained for those ten years. His government had succeeded in a neo-liberalization of the common opinion – an ideological turn that had made values such as personal freedom and individual choice the premises of the debate.

The Opening Address

According to Article 38 of the Danish Constitution, the Prime Minister must "render an account of the general state of the country and of the measures proposed by the Government" on the first assembly of the Danish parliament each year.[41] The oral statement is followed by a written report of the government's bills. In the early days of Danish democracy, the Opening Address was reminiscent of the king's throne speech, but with the constitution of 1953, the duty passed to the Prime Minister. As early as 1925, however, Prime Minister Thorvald Stauning founded the tradition of giving a political speech on behalf of the government on the first day of the assembly.[42]

The idea of an annual political address was imported from the United States, where a State of the Union Address had been institutionalized since 1913.[43] Early in the century, the American speech was known as the annual message, but in 1949 it took its name from the American Constitution's Article 2, Section 3, which specifies that the president "shall from time to time give to the Congress information on the state of the Union and recommend to their consideration such measures as he shall judge necessary and expedient."[44]

A comparative glance at American rhetorical critics Karlyn Kohrs Campbell and Kathleen Hall Jamieson's generic study of the State of the Union Address will be helpful. Campbell and Jamieson have detected three elements that reveal the functions of the State of the Union Address: 1) Assessments of information and issues, 2) Policy rec-

---

41 "At the first meeting in the sessional year the Prime Minister shall render an account of the general state of the country and of the measures proposed by the Government. Such account shall be made the subject of a general debate." Article 38 in The Constitutional Act of Denmark of June 5, 1953. See also Marie Lund Klujeff, "Folketingets åbningstaler, 1953-" http://danmarkshistorien.dk/leksikon-og-kilder/vis/materiale/folketingets-aabningstaler-1953/?no_cache=1&cHash=88118ae48ecfc8d91ffdaa00f60e9bee.

42 Peter Heyn Nielsen has documented the existence of the speech as far back as 1850, although it does not gain statutory power in the constitution until 1953. Peter Heyn Nielsen, "Statsministeren fik ordet – historien om den danske åbningstale," *Økonomi og politik* 85 (2012).

43 Tim Knudsen, "Statsministeren har ordet," *Information*, October 5, 2009.

44 Karlyn Kohrs Campbell & Kathleen Hall Jamieson, *Presidents Creating the Presidency. Deeds Done in Words*, (Chicago: University of Chicago Press, 2008), 136.

ommendations that follow from the assessments, and 3) Public meditations on values.[45] The Danish Opening Address is characterized by the same elements, as I shall show. My study then turns to Prime Minister Helle Thorning-Schmidt's first Opening Address and the question of style as a key to understanding political rhetoric and influence.

According to Campbell and Jamieson, the State of the Union Address often establishes a link between the two first elements: the president's interpretation of problems and the political propositions. The president is given the opportunity to launch a comprehensive narrative and, on this basis, to chart a course for the nation. Or, as Campbell and Jamieson put it: "the Constitution offers [the presidents] the role of national historian, giving them the opportunity to reconstruct the past in order to forge the future. [...] The more eloquent presidents have seized the opportunity to reshape reality and to imprint their conception of it on the nation."[46]

Almost the same generic texture can be found in the Danish Opening Address. The formulation in the Danish Constitution – "to render an account of the general state of the country and of the measures proposed by the Government" – linguistically ties the Prime Minister's interpretation of the state of the nation closely to the government's political proposals. The purpose of the Opening Address therefore is less to account for existing problems in a transparent and fitting language, than to create a collective narrative that may serve as the ideational point of departure for future initiatives.

Like the State of the Union Address, the Danish Opening Address is characterized by a meditation on values. Stock topics are: praise of the Constitution, praise of Danish democracy, and, especially, praise of the collaboration of the Danish parliament.[47] Frequently, this epi-

---

45 Campbell & Jamieson, *President Creating the Presidency*, 139. For my own purpose, I have reversed the order of the three elements.

46 Ibid., 137.

47 Collaboration is needed in the Danish parliament because the government is most often in the minority.

deictic element is also used to reflect on and re-interpret what it means to be Danish. The interpretation of Danish identity clearly has an argumentative function. The Opening Address is a political speech, and the construction of a national collective identity is used to back political propositions.

One example of how the construction of a national collective identity is used to warrant political dispositions is found in the social democratic Prime Minister Jens Otto Krag's Opening Address of 1972. The Address was given the day after the Danish election, when a majority of Danes voted yes to join the European Economic Community. In the speech, Krag performed the role of national historian as he inscribed the Danish history in a narration of a unique European identity. To account for the purpose of the Danish membership of the European Economic Community, he re-established European kinship by drawing connections with the cradle of democracy:

> We want to maintain and develop the democracy as it was born in the European continent, and as it was developed differently according to the will and thoughts of the nations and of the people. [...] Let us make use of the new Europe to create a continent that unites the best of European culture – from ancient Hellas and Rome to the modern times that we live in ourselves.[48]

The construction of national character is embedded in the national narrative. A distinct example is found in the Opening Address from 2002, when Danish citizens were given an identity as quality-conscious consumers. The general storyline was the government's desire to optimize the Danish welfare system to provide a good service to citizens.

---

48 Jens Otto Krag, Opening Address, October 3, 1972. My translation. http://danmarkshistorien.dk/leksikon-og-kilder/vis/materiale/jens-otto-krags-s-tale-ved-folketingets-aabning-1972/?no_cache=1&cHash=c90ba371e59c1de84015c20fcd07050a.

According to the liberalist Prime Minister Anders Fogh Rasmussen, it was of utmost importance that "we as citizens" got the highest level of quality for our money.[49]

Both the collective narrative and the construction of a collective identity are strong threads in the Opening Address of 2011. The first female Prime Minister, Helle Thorning-Schmidt, presented a kickstart of growth as the government's answer to the financial crisis. The Danish nation was to work its way of out the crisis, and the relationship between the government and the citizens was to be a working one. Drawing on core social democratic values, she wove this into a story about the need for collaboration and partnership.[50]

The Prime Minister's Style

The speech made by Prime Minister Helle Thorning-Schmidt on the first assembly of the Danish parliament in 2011 fully meets the requirements of the genre. Its assessment of the state of the country gives presence to unequivocal formulations of a financial crisis and its implications: "Danish industries have lost jobs in tens of thousands. It is hard on the unemployed. It is difficult for families. And it will cost society dearly."[51] The interpretation of a crisis, however, serves as the point of departure for a narrative about advance and improvement: "After stagnation the time has come for progress and change." Thus, the government's intended actions are to lead Denmark out of the

---

49 Anders Fogh Rasmussen, Opening Address, October 1, 2002. http://danmarkshistorien.dk/leksikon-og-kilder/vis/materiale/anders-fogh-rasmussens-v-tale-ved-folketingets-aabning-2002/?no_cache=1&cHash=6c3da8f2aa8d82c136cbcb6f4b5b2f71

50 Helle Thorning-Schmidt, Opening Address, October 4, 2011, http://www.stm.dk/_p_13517.html.

51 Thorning-Schmidt, Opening Address. My translation.

crisis by advancing public investments: "We shall put a stop to negative development. We shall restore faith in the future."[52]

When explaining the concrete measurements such as a reform of taxes and activation of the unemployed, Helle Thorning-Schmidt ties an ideologically based interpretation of the problems to the solution offered by the government: "A balanced economy forms the basis of a Denmark in progress. And of a Denmark without vast social differences. Therefore, a responsible economic policy is crucial to the government."

The ideology of solidarity and equality is reinforced in the third element that characterizes the genre: the construction of values that define the imagined Danish community. The national identity offered by Thorning-Schmidt is one of collaborative engagement: "We must build our future on strong communities." This idea of a collaborative society, in fact, is the common thread in her Opening Address. In the conclusion, she appoints collaboration as not merely the government's preferred policy, but the *only* answer to the present crisis: "Denmark has a new government. A government which aims to create a new cooperation for Denmark. Because only by cooperating can we steer Denmark through the hard times ahead of us. Only by encouraging us to come together can we secure the welfare of our children and grandchildren." Although key terms like "solidarity" are used very sparingly, synonyms more palatable to a contemporary audience – such as "cooperation" and "collaboration" ("samarbejde"), "partnership" ("partnerskab") and "community" ("fællesskab") – are used frequently. Far from a random choice of wording, this indeed looks like a rhetorical strategy. It also looks like a rhetorical style.

In terms of rhetorical leadership, Helle Thorning-Schmidt has been characterized on the one hand as a great speaker who has nothing to say, and on the other, as a leader who makes other people heard. In the last and positive interpretation, she makes debating worthwhile,

52 Ibid.

because she allows herself to be influenced by strong arguments. She does not fight for her own position, but engages in deliberation in order to find the best solution. In the first, negative interpretation, Helle Thorning-Schmidt is a political leader with no political stance. To her, nothing is more important than anything else. From this viewpoint, she is a cynical opportunist who is able to speak emphatically and convincingly about policies that she does not believe in.[53]

The two views on Thorning-Schmidt's rhetorical accomplishments seem to perfectly cohere with the traditional topoi of style. From one angle, she is a brilliant speaker (in itself a suspicious feature, it seems) who masters the art of speaking persuasively, even about issues and policies that she does not support. The style she displays is technically superb and *kairotic*; it is tuned to acquire power and solve problems. It is an effective and elocutionary, yet superficial and empty, style coincident with the topos of style as dress. The more positive view, conversely, coheres with topoi where style is understood to incarnate some essential quality: style as man or style as political culture. It calls attention to the fact that Thorning-Schmidt's style not only reflects her personality, but also a political culture at large. From this angle, her rhetorical style is defined by her willingness to listen to other people's opinions and to be persuaded by good arguments. It is a style that is so oriented towards consensus in problem resolution that key political issues may easily be overruled.[54]

My own reading is based on the third topos of style. Emphasizing a collective narrative, I interpret her style as constitutive of collaboration. It is a constitutive style that creates the qualities, ethics, and aesthetics of cooperation rhetorically, in its practice. In line with Vivian's idea of "a rhetoric of collective style", her style constitutes the new values, ethics, and sentiments rhetorically in her narrative about partnership and community among Danes. In this style, politics is no

---

53 Rune Lykkeberg, "Statsministerens stil," *Information*, January 6, 2012.

54 Ibid.

fait accompli, but must be made as we go along, in a dialog between the citizens and the leader of the state. According to this understanding of politics, deliberation and process are important components for decision-making that shape not only the society, but also the citizens-as-partners.

The communal style of Helle Thorning-Schmidt communicates collaboration on the Danish project. She invites individual subjects to be active participants and partners in shaping Danish society and taking responsibility for its continued growth. The goal of it all is within our reach: to secure free and equal access to the health system. When articulating the common objective, a rare metaphor marks a change of style as she announces free and equal access to be "the crown jewel of the welfare society."

The aim of my rhetorical analysis has been to investigate the critical possibilities of 'postmodern style' in relation to core political practice. While the prevailing theories on the topic are adjusted to the identity formations of sub-cultures or counter-audiences, my quest has been to develop constitutive style as a critical concept that can also be used to understand the rhetoric of high politics. In the case of Helle Thorning-Schmidt, it offers an explanation for the government's rhetorical failure. While it was obvious that her personal style and the political style of the party never came to function as a cohesive cluster, the real problem seemed to lie elsewhere: that her collaborative style was never a counter-narrative strong enough to rearticulate the neo-liberalization of the common opinion.

SUB-CONCLUSION

According to Wolfgang G. Müller, the two topoi "style as man" and "style as dress" are competitive in their view on style and language. In the former, style is inextricably linked with the individual personality; in the latter, style is an added form which dresses an already available thought. Furthermore, the topos of style as dress is associated with social skills such as good manners, a cultured lifestyle, a sense of decorum, and eloquence. Based on a garment metaphor, it offers a perspective on style as a social phenomenon. A *kairotic* ability to read a situation and deliver an appropriate performance in response is important when style is understood as dress. *Aptum* rules, so to speak. The topos is decisive in Neoclassical theories of style; yet, according to Müller, it also coheres with the concept of *elocutio*.

The topos of style as man, on the other hand, designates a perfect union of the speaker's character and oral skills. It is present in the Roman ideal of *vir bonus*, a good man who speaks well, but it gains further territory in early Romanticism, in which style is understood as a key to the human being in its unique individuality. Additionally, it embraces notions of style as the spirit of an epoch, the spirit of a national identity, or an incarnation of an idea. In the topos of style as man, authenticity rules.

In chapter one, discussing Müller's development of the two stylistic topoi, I proposed a third topos: constitutive rhetorical style. This converges neither with social and ornamental nor referential qualities; rather, it sees style as constitutive of thought, argumentation, social relations, communicative action, identity, and gender. A similar interpretation of style as sign can be found in the development of metaphor. Twentieth-century theories view metaphor as generative of a new meaning: The effect produced by the metaphor can no longer be regarded as an addition of feeling and value. Nor can metaphor be reduced to a mere supplement of lucidity or muscle. A metaphor is not just a stronger, more pleasing, or more memorable expression of a thought otherwise untouched. It alters the thought in a fundamental sense and constructs meanings in new ways.

Indisputably, modern theories of metaphor have succeeded in releasing the cognitive and creative potential of metaphors. Metaphor's ability to shape and frame the course of political debates or crisis communication, for instance, has become common knowledge, and it is today used strategically by parliamentary politicians to frame the political debate. In various academic fields, metaphor is a key concept in the analysis and interpretation of diverse discourse types such as poetry, narratives of the self, cognitive psychology, organizational communication, and political speeches. Therefore, to argue the case that the much larger reservoir of rhetorical figures holds a similar cognitive potential does not seem insurmountable. However, a conclusion of this sort comes up against a default attitude present in rhetorical manuals old and new: Rhetorical figures belong to a special domain of figured language, they are deviations from a more common, normal, or literal usage, and therefore they function as additions of value or feeling to the message.

Rhetoric critic Jeanne Fahnestock has refuted this standard approach to rhetorical figures. She has delivered a thorough argument that some rhetorical figures have the ability to structure, shape, and frame argumentation and reasoning. In her investigation of a handful of rhetorical figures she moves the discussion of what has traditionally been perceived as *elocutio* towards the topos of *inventio*. In fact, her thesis that some rhetorical figures are epitomized arguments is written in explicit opposition to an understanding of rhetorical figures as an added quality. In Müller's terms we can identify her adversary position as the topos of style as dress.

The topos of constitutive style is developed from a theory of constitutive rhetoric, which among its various agendas includes a critique of the transcendent subject. In the topos of constitutive style, textuality is considered fundamental to being and behavior. Like the theory of constitutive rhetoric, constitutive style is reflected on in terms of its productive and inventive potential. It is the creator of identity, ideas, arguments, and values in a strategic sense: how one wants to appear and be perceived by others, or how one sets the agenda or gains terminological control in argument and deliberation. But style is more than an intentional strategy used by an autonomous agent to desired ends. Constitutive style in many instances testifies to the social character of the individual. Drawing on the idea that the individual exists in and is shaped by particular social contexts in which discursive and aesthetic practices are formative of values and norms, I turn constitutive style into a rhetorical critical concept. Style becomes an analytical focus we can use to describe how subjects function collectively. Rhetorical discourse and behavior is analyzed with a focus on how it is used to act politically, how subjects become audiences, and how audiences form their opinions. Thus, analysis of style, taste, and aesthetic judgment will allow us to observe how individuals get to know themselves as groups through their shared aesthetic preferences.

In part one, I developed the three stylistic topoi in analyses of different cases. For instance, I showed how a critical essay on the style of a Danish Minister of Culture was founded on a perception of style as social rank and propriety. Its mockery of a minister who had the appearance of a cultured person and therefore could do nothing wrong in the eyes of the cultural elite was identified as the topos of style as dress. Yet simultaneously, the topos of style as man was implied in a contrasting reading of the minister's style as a sign of cultural and political competence. As an alternative to these traditional topoi, I introduced style as constitutive of identity and political action. This perspective offered a third interpretation of style as a bricolage of past merits and political decisions used to form a new homology – a new stylistic order. Different political contexts were carefully combined to work together and reinvent the minister's public persona. The purpose of this stylistic strategy was to make possible a radical production of a public character that would give him a specific political agency as well as rid him of a tarnished reputation.

Similar productive qualities of style were the carriers of a study of a magnificently orchestrated collective style resulting in a shared sense of national identity. Rather than interpreting the sartorial Scottish rhetoric traditionally as style as dress, Brummett stressed its re-invention of highland society and its successful re-inscription of the king as a member of a unique culture. I transferred some of these critical insights into a reading of the Danish Opening Address, where a collective narrative of national values and identity served as the ideational point of departure for future initiatives. The topos of constitutive style offered a perspective on the Danish Prime Minister Helle Thorning-Schmidt's rhetorical style as constitutive of collaboration. Her style was interpreted as an attempt to constitute values of partnership and community rhetorically. In her constitutive narrative, political action was created in the course of public conversation.

Some methodological and pedagogical perspectives of my critical approach deserve elaboration. My readings of different rhetorical artefacts reveal that it is often both possible and analytically productive to test all three stylistic topoi, and meticulously to puzzle out their interpretative perspectives. When the analysis of the different topoi falls into place, a three-facetted reflection on style is available. The contrast of these interpretative lines allows the critic to see through some of the presumptions on language, style, aesthetics, and politics that govern argumentation and rhetorical discourse. Furthermore, it enables her to form her own opinion and criticize the prevailing taste and attitude. It also adds to the development and understanding of style.

Still, although I acknowledge that the three topoi are living parts of our common vocabulary, I do not find all three topoi to be equally significant. I favor an understanding of style as a constitutive practice which brings about its ideas or values in discursive or performative ways. Because I both recognize the existence of three prevailing notions of style and find that one is more valid than others, I find it crucial to maintain a conceptual stringency: to insist that it matters which topos a particular formulation of style and rhetorical figures is tied to. The likely outcome of an erratic course of terminology is not only theoretical confusion, but also communicative and pedagogical inexpedience. If students and critics simply fall back on common assumptions in their description of the function of style and rhetorical figures, it will be hard to put the theoretical perspectives of constitutive style into analytical and critical practice.

The critical perspectives of style, especially constitutive style, are at the center of Part Two. While many styles already considered (intercultural style, conversational style, republican style, and bureaucratic style, to name a few) could have served as relevant and interesting objects, I have limited my critical study to elaborated studies of three aspects of style. Chapter four studies the feminine style, a term originally developed by Karlyn Kohrs Campbell. The feminine style functions as a coherent repertoire which traditionally prescribed the social code of conduct for female public speaking. However, when transported into contemporary Danish local politics, the value and agency of this stylistic order seem to have undergone a fundamental change. In chapter five I develop my own concept of a particular style, the provocative style, in the study of a heated debate. Chapter six explores some of the aspects of style that have occupied rhetorical critics of speechwriting, especially the aspect of 'ethopoeia'. Unlike the chapters it succeeds, this last exploration is not a close reading of rhetorical practice, but a critical discussion of concepts that may, in turn, be used in practice.

PART II

Critical Perspectives

CHAPTER FOUR

FEMININE STYLE IN DANISH LOCAL POLITICS

This chapter studies feminine style in a debate between local politicians in the city of Aarhus. The debate was part of a campaign organized by the Ministry for Gender Equality to encourage more women to run for the municipal elections in 2009. The investigation falls into three parts: Firstly, I trace the theoretical development of the concept of feminine style in American rhetorical criticism, especially in regard to the ways in which the concept has been shaped by consistent lines of definition as well as inherent conflicts. Historically, the feminine style has been a persuasive strategy used by women to secure themselves a speaking position in a male dominated society, but its contemporary use and function is more disputed. Some rhetorical critics perceive of feminine style as empowering, and as a critique of traditional grounds for political judgment. Other rhetorical critics argue that the feminine style is a limiting and potentially reactionary strategy.

Secondly, I transfer the concept to a Danish context and focus attention on its specific strategic components. Historical Danish rhetorical artifacts evince an ample and expedient use of the feminine style, as documented by a speech on women's right to vote and be elected by the Danish feminist Gyrithe Lemche in 1908. I analyze this speech in order to isolate some features that are essential to the successful use of the feminine style. The extracted features are later drawn on in a comparison with audience constructions in the Aarhus debate example.

Thirdly, I interpret the debate case and its perspectives. The feminine style seems to be a way for politicians to argue qualitatively, on the grounds of women's particular skills, interests, experiences, and discursive strategies, for more women to join local politics. In doing so, however, the debaters' performance of the feminine style constitutes the audience as women with traditional values and a restricted set of possibilities. As this is unlikely to be a public norm in contemporary Danish society, I question the impact as well as the expedience of this rhetorical strategy.

The Concept of "Feminine Style"

Although Karlyn Kohrs Campbell does not use the term *feminine style* in "The Rhetoric of Women's Liberation: An Oxymoron" (1973), stylistic features are central to this early and influential study of feminist rhetoric. Campbell examines the rhetoric of women's liberation as a genre which fuses substantive and stylistic features.[1] Stylistically, the rhetoric of women's liberation is distinctive from a traditional understanding of rhetoric as public persuasion. It addresses its audience of oppressed women in terms of their private, concrete, and individual experience in order to enhance awareness that their individual problems are also common and shared. The persuasive means are centered on qualities such as "affirmation of the affective, of the validity of personal experience, of the necessity for self-exposure and

1 In this study, Campbell defines style rather broadly as a body of characteristics in a persuasive campaign: "In addition to the linguistic features usually considered, the stylistic features of a persuasive campaign include, in my view, characteristic modes of rhetorical interaction, typical ways of structuring the relationships among participants in a rhetorical transaction, and emphasis on particular forms of argument, proof, and evidence." Karlyn Kohrs Campbell, "The Rhetoric of Women's Liberation: An Oxymoron," in *Contemporary Rhetorical Theory*, ed. John Louis Lucaites et al. (New York: The Guilford Press, 1999), 400.

self-criticism, of the value of dialogue, and of the goal of autonomous, individual decision making."[2]

Despite the concern for the individual perspective, the aim of women's liberation rhetoric is to make women realize that singular problems have social and structural origins. Campbell states that in the process of "consciousness raising," the personal must be transcended by moving toward the political: that in fact, unless such transcendence occurs, there is no rhetoric in any public sense.[3] On the other hand, the fusion of substantive and stylistic features cannot be reduced to a matter of expedience. The goal of women's liberation rhetoric is a process of subverting traditional norms and values, and of radically reconstructing identity. Campbell concludes that the oxymoron is the rhetorical figure which best sums up the paradoxes of women's liberation rhetoric: "Rhetoric is usually defined as dealing with public issues, structural analyses, and social action, yet women's liberation emphasizes acts concerned with personal exigencies and private, concrete experience and its goal is frequently limited to particular, autonomous action by individuals."[4]

In a later study, *Man Cannot Speak for Her* (1989), which is a historical restoration of early feminist rhetoric in America, Campbell outlines the concept of "feminine style," which she defines as a rhetorical strategy:

> Analysis of persuasion by women indicates that many strategically adopted what might be called a feminine style to cope with the conflicting demands of the podium. That style emerged out of their experiences as women and was adapted to the attitudes and experiences of female audiences. However,

---

2 Ibid.

3 Ibid., 404.

4 Ibid., 405.

> it was not, and is not today, a style exclusive to women, either as speakers or as audiences.[5]

As a persuasive strategy, feminine style consists of a set of characteristics resembling those outlined in the earlier article. Discourses applying feminine style will be personal in tone (relying on personal experience, anecdotes, and examples), invite audience participation, and address audience members as peers with recognition of authority based on experience. The discourse seeks to induce empowerment and to persuade women who have been subdued by traditional concepts of womanhood – passivity, submissiveness, and patience – that they can act.[6]

The critical reception of the concept of feminine style has taken different directions. Most notably, some studies favor the concept as holding potential for liberation, while others suspect that a gender-oriented rhetorical style will turn out to be limiting. A positive stance is taken by Bonnie J. Dow and Mari Boor Tonn in their reading of the rhetoric of the Texas Governor Ann Richards, which they believe has radical implications: "in her rhetoric, feminine style functions not only as a strategy for audience empowerment but as a critique of traditional grounds for political judgment."[7] Emphasizing Richards' use of personal anecdote and concrete examples, they find a "potential for feminine style to function philosophically as well as strategically, by creating alternative grounds for testing the validity claims for public knowledge."[8] The characteristics of feminine style thus work to promote an alternative political philosophy reflecting

---

5 Karlyn Kohrs Campbell, *Man Cannot Speak for Her 1-2. Contributions in Women's Studies* 101 (Westport: Greenwood Press, 1989), 12.

6 Ibid., 13.

7 Bonnie J. Dow & Mari Boor Tonn, "'Feminine Style' and Political Judgment in the Rhetoric of Ann Richards," *The Quarterly Journal of Speech* 79, 3 (1993): 287.

8 Ibid., 291.

feminine values.[9] Jane Blankenship and Deborah C. Robson, who understand feminine style as "comprised of the dimensions of discourse which may reveal or point to epistemic stances which we discover in the public political discourse of women," take a similar standpoint.[10] Slightly altering Campbell's concept, Blankenship and Robson identify five characteristics of feminine style: "These include: basing political judgments on concrete, lived experience, valuing inclusivity and the relational nature of being; conceptualizing the power of public office as a capacity to 'get things done' and to empower others; approaching policy formation holistically; and, moving women's issues to the forefront of the public arena."[11]

According to Shawn J. Parry-Giles and Trevor Parry-Giles, such celebration may be too hasty, and their own investigations indicate that the influence of feminine style is potentially reactionary. In a study of feminine style in presidential campaign films (Reagan, G. Bush, Dukakis, B. Clinton), they reach a conclusion contrary to that of previous studies of feminine style: "Instead of resulting in a feminized politic sphere, contemporary campaign rhetorics reflect the continual marginalization of women in the political process and the general exclusion of women from political office and political power."[12] Parry-Giles and Parry-Giles argue that in the campaign films feminine style is employed both in the presentation of the "masculine"

---

9 Ibid., 287. James Jasinski has suggested that Dow and Tonn's discussion of feminine style and political judgment holds the potentially provocative thesis that feminine style is an unconscious recuperation of a Classical Aristotelian tradition of practical philosophy centered on prudence, *phronesis*, and social knowledge. James Jasinski, *Sourcebook on Rhetoric. Key Concepts in Contemporary Rhetorical Studies* (Thousand Oaks: Sage Publications, 2001), 255.

10 Jane Blankenship & Deborah C. Robson, "A 'Feminine Style' in Women's Political Discourse: An Exploratory Essay," *Communication Quarterly* 43, 3 (1995): 357.

11 Ibid., 353.

12 Shawn Parry-Giles & Trevor Parry-Giles, "Gendered Politics and Presidential Image Construction: A Reassessment of the 'Feminine Style'," *Communication Monographs* 63 (1996): 338.

and "presidential" character of the candidate and in the constructions of the women.[13] In a study of the use of feminine style in presidential campaign discourse from 1960 to 2000, based on quantitative content analysis, Danette Ifert Johnson concludes that presidential debaters have tended to use elements of feminine style less over time. [14] This observation also lends some support to Parry-Giles and Parry-Giles' doubt that feminine style influences the general opinion on a more philosophical level.

In a more recent article, "The Discursive Performance of Femininity: Hating Hillary" (1998), Campbell has re-launched feminine style in a study of Hillary Clinton's rhetorical strategy as first lady. The study tips towards a less celebratory evaluation of the function of feminine style. It is Campbell's thesis that Hillary Clinton's immense unpopularity was to some degree caused by her failure to live up to the societal standards for public female behavior. Those standards are summed up in an elaborated concept of "feminine rhetorical style," which is theoretically based on a feminist distinction between sex versus gender, as well as Judith Butler's theory of gender as performance and behavior: "it is enacted and performed bodily, and in order for a 'woman' or 'girl' to be an agent, to assume what postmodernists call the 'subject position' [...] she must 'cite' or 'enact' cultural norms of femininity."[15]

Campbell finds a parallel to the attacks on Hillary Clinton in the nineteenth-century controversies about female dress codes. In con-

---

13 Parry-Giles and Parry-Giles observe that the portrayal of Hillary Clinton in the Bill Clinton campaign film *The Man from Hope* represents "the most telling evidence of the gendered construction of women in these films. Unlike her husband, who is allowed to speak about family *and* politics, Hillary Clinton has a voice only on issues relating to the family." Ibid., 347.

14 Danette Ifert Johnson, "Feminine Style in Presidential Debate Discourse, 1960-2000," *Communication Quarterly* 53, 1 (2005): 16.

15 Karlyn Kohrs Campbell, "The Discursive Performance of Femininity: Hating Hillary," *Rhetoric & Public Affairs* 1, 1 (1998): 2. Judith P. Butler, *Gender Trouble* (New York: Routledge, 1990).

tinuation of her earlier studies, she emphasizes the strategic paradox that faced women who were to speak in public:

> What can be summed up as "feminine rhetorical style" were strategic responses by nineteenth-century women to two competing sets of cultural norms: gender norms for the performance of femininity and rhetorical norms governing public advocacy. Put simply, women speakers were expected to reaffirm their womanliness discursively at the same time that they demonstrated the ordinary rhetorical competencies – cogent argument, clarity of position, offering compelling evidence, and responding to competing views – that were gender-coded as masculine.[16]

According to Campbell, this conflict persists although it has been modified through time, and her study of Clinton supports this claim insofar that Clinton's neglect of the feminine style is a direct downside of the excellent rhetorical skills she has developed as a lawyer and now exercises in political argument. Campbell's revised description of the concrete features of feminine style draws on her two earlier studies; as the elaborated description of the characteristics of feminine style form the basis of the rhetorical analysis of the Danish debate that follows, I cite it in full:

> In rhetorical terms, performing or enacting femininity has meant adopting a personal or self-disclosing tone (signifying nurturance, intimacy, and domesticity) and assuming a feminine persona, e.g., mother, or an ungendered persona, e.g., mediator or prophet, while speaking. It has meant preferring anecdotal evidence (reflecting women's experiential learning in contrast to men's expertise), developing ideas inductively (so

16 Campbell, "The Discursive Performance of Femininity," 4.

> the audience thinks that it, not this presumptuous woman, drew the conclusions), and appropriating strategies associated with women – such as domestic metaphors, emotional appeals to motherhood, and the like – and avoiding such 'macho' strategies as tough language, confrontation or direct refutation, and any appearance of debating one's opponents. Note, however, that feminine style does not preclude substantive depth and argumentative cogency.[17]

So far, this small, selective survey of the criticism of feminine style confirms that the body of characteristics remains fairly consistent. Thus, Hillary Clinton's failure to live up to the norms for female public speaking leads to Campbell's blame of society rather than her: "Judged purely in terms of achieving her goals [...], her limited ability to feminize her rhetorical style, to perform a culturally defined role publicly, is clearly a disadvantage. At the same time, our failure to appreciate the highly developed argumentative skills of an expert advocate, when that advocate is a female, reveals our deficiencies, not hers."[18]

To summarize the discussions among American rhetorical critics, many critics believe the feminine style to have a liberating potential, not least when viewed from a historical perspective as a feminized rhetorical strategy aimed at an audience of suppressed women. Moreover, the feminine style is acknowledged, historically, for having secured a speaking position for female rhetors. Thus, as a rhetorical strategy tailored for women's specific constraints and possibilities in the nineteenth century, it is esteemed for its ability to give agency to women as orators. Performed in a modern or postmodern setting, however, some critics have found it potentially reactionary as it reflects and perpetuates a stagnated, suppressive norm for female behavior. Other

17 Ibid., 5.

18 Ibid., 15.

critics have seen in the feminine style a rhetorical strategy also capable of giving agency to contemporary female speakers; by some, it is even ascribed an ability to subvert traditional norms for public deliberation and judgment.

Feminine Style in Early Danish Liberation Discourse

Before turning to a close reading of the Danish debate example, I shall argue for the importance of feminine style in early Danish democracy. Historically, women's rights came to the fore in two periods, 1870-1920 and 1970-1985. Besides women's right to vote, some of the key issues in the late nineteenth century were equal rights in education and the job market. In the last quarter of the nineteenth century, Danish women began to organize in women's societies and in the international suffrage movement. In 1908, Danish women gained the right to vote for the municipal councils, and in 1915 the right to be elected to the national parliament. In the second wave of the feminist movement, many of the old key issues were revisited while new ones, such as free abortion, were added.

Besides the right to vote, the feminists were of course involved in other political issues. One example is a debate about sexual morality ("Sædelighedsfejden"), which engaged both feminists and Scandinavian intellectuals. The debate was initiated by a play, "En Handske" (1883), by the Norwegian author Bjørnstjerne Bjørnson. Taking the side of Bjønson, the conservative members of the feminist movement held that men, like women, should practice sexual abstinence before marriage. On the other hand, a number of writers, feminists, and intellectuals attacked the bourgeois hypocrisy of this, and argued in favor of sexual emancipation for both sexes.

In the first years of the Danish women's rights movement, the activists found themselves in a rhetorical dilemma. In order to influence political action, they had to argue their case potently and poignantly. Simultaneously, in order to influence public opinion they could not too obviously violate a norm for female behavior that prescribed modesty and restraint. Feminine style was the perfect answer to this situational challenge, as illustrated by an address made at a women's society's meeting on the right to vote. In this speech, the Danish feminist Gyrithe Lemche performs the feminine style with great expedience, as she combines it with less meek rhetorical modes.

Taken as a whole, the speech is a counterargument to the reasons given by the members of the Danish parliament Rigsdagen for not granting women political influence. Lemche deconstructs the implied dichotomy between men and women with a list of differences between women. Allegedly accepting the accusations of women's political immaturity in the beginning of the speech, a fierce irony is soon unmistakable. The argument culminates when she, on behalf of the women's rights movement, offers to advise men on the organization of a political movement once they have matured politically. Rhetorically, she grants herself and other women the agency they deserve: "We women's rights women, so many or so few that we are, grant ourselves political maturity [...]."[19]

Gyrithe Lemche's speech, however, also evinces a careful performance of feminine style. In a crucial metaphor, the feminist movement is associated with violent forces of nature (a river, a fire), but when the metaphor is first introduced, it is in the shape of a tree of freedom which grows in an old pot. The feminist movement is the necessary new soil in the pot. A similar domestic metaphor is found in a more elaborate comparison that also revives the idea of political maturity: "When children have outgrown their clothing, new clothing is needed, otherwise they will tear up the clothes, and that was bad economy, as all good housewives know. But, when we women have outgrown the once given frames, new frames are certainly needed as

19 Gyrithe Lemche, Speech at Dansk Kvindesamfund's meeting on the right to vote, Rosenborg Have, June 28, 1908. My translation. http://danmarkshistorien.dk/leksikon-og-kilder/vis/materiale/gyrithe-lemches-tale-ved-valgretsmoede-i-rosenborg-have-28-juni-1908/?no_cache=1.

well, otherwise we will tear up the old – and that is bad economy by the political housewives."[20]

Undoubtedly, the allusions to household budgeting and bringing up children corresponded to the experience of many women in the audience. By citing the feminine style, Lemche thus constituted her audience more widely than if she had only addressed the committed few who already considered themselves feminists. Lemche's speech is a powerful instance of a strategic use of feminine style: a rhetoric that re-inscribes women who understand themselves mainly as mothers, wives, maids, or housewives into a narrative that allows them to view themselves as political subjects. Its success seems to be the result of a careful braiding of conflicting interests – a more traditional representation of women's role with a new consciousness of women's potential to influence public matters.

The Debate in Aarhus City Hall

A century later, the celebration of the hundredth anniversary of Danish women's right to vote and run in municipal elections gave rise to a campaign issued by the Ministry of Gender Equality.[21] The campaign consisted of a variety of initiatives – a debate, a leaflet, and a brunch meeting – with the goal of encouraging more women to run for the elections in November 2009. The need for action was evident; while 38 percent of the national parliament and 37 percent of the government were women in 2007, female representation in local town councils did not exceed 27 percent. This difference between women's representation in the national parliament and municipal councils is a fact of history, and it persists to the present day. To explain this, election experts have pointed to, among other factors, the recruiting practice of the parties' local chapters and the poor working conditions for local politicians.

20 Ibid.

21 In 1909, the first Danish women were elected to municipal councils.

In contrast to the situation in Denmark, the representation of women in national and local politics in other Scandinavian countries has reached over 40 percent.[22]

When the campaign was launched, Aarhus, which is the second largest city in Denmark, was statistically average, with only eight female council members out of a total of thirty-one, or about one quarter of the city council. The hundredth anniversary, March 12, 2009, was marked with an event in the city hall: an amateur theatre play and a subsequent debate about female representation in the city council. Participating in the panel debate were six members of the current city council; the majority were party spokespersons on gender equality, and five out of the six were women.[23] Lotte Hansen, a female commentator on political communication, and publicly known from a weekly television program about political spin, chaired the debate. After the play about the first two women to be elected to Aarhus City Council, in 1909, the meeting opened with an anecdote about the young and popular male mayor, Nicolai Wammen, who had blessed the initiative with the ambiguous message that more women in local politics was a cause worth fighting for – he just hoped that they did not take his seat!

After a round of introductions focusing on the politicians' stance on equality issues as well as on their own experience of the barriers to entering local politics, the chair informed the audience that a list of concrete priorities was to be produced over the following few hours. Two rounds of responses followed; firstly, the politicians were to respond "yes" or "no" to the question "Is it important to have more women in Aarhus City Council?" and secondly, they were to com-

---

22 Anette Borchhorst, "27 procent kvinder i dansk lokalpolitik – hvad er problemet?," in *Kvinder i kommunalpolitik 1909-2009. Festskrift for 100 år med kvinders valgret*, ed. Jytte Larsen (2009), http://kvinfo.dk/2015/kvinder-i-kommunalpolitik-1909-2009-festskrift-100-aar-med-kvinders-valgret.

23 Dansk Folkeparti, a medium-sized, right-leaning party with strong national values, was not represented on the panel.

ment on whether female representation makes a difference in political work. In general, the politicians answered in the affirmative, although some expressed cautiousness, or ambivalence, in regard to the actual impact of gender on decision-making. The chair, Lotte Hansen, had the politicians make concrete suggestions for what could be done to increase female representation. Suggestions included secretarial support and meetings during working hours instead of in the evening and at dinner-time. Once the politicians had commented on the list of suggestions, the audience was allowed to pose questions.

I will carry out the rhetorical analysis of this case as a close reading of one particular question posed by a female member of the audience, and of the answers it provoked. Contrary to most of the discussion that evening, this question evoked answers about principles and ideas. Of special concern to this study, it also produced some distinct markers of feminine style. Below I cite the question and the answers in full:[24]

> Lotte Hansen. We'll just take one more comment here …
>
> Citizen: I would like to return to the beginning … it says here in the program: "More women in the city council – why and how", and we have been talking a lot about how and about meal times and … ah … s-secretary help and this and that … If you are to motivate me, and, I guarantee, a whole lot of others, to run then you will have to make it clear to me why it is important. It is as if you're just assuming that it is important to have a lot of women in politics, and I think that you got off lightly with this debate about values …

---

24 Recorded and cited with the permission of Aarhus City Hall administration. The transcription does not adhere to a specific method with a developed notation system, but is simply a transcription of words and pauses. The transcription and translation are mine. To keep the record straight, the person who asked the question is a teacher of rhetoric and a colleague of mine. In the debate, however, she interacts as a citizen and is therefore designated as such.

Lotte Hansen: Yes …

Citizen: … which I somehow think it is. Why? What is it that we can do? What kind of values do we contribute? What is it that women as such contribute? Should we also have … ah … more handicapped … more … ah … something … what do I know? Where … what is it … why is it important besides the fact that … that … 50 percent of us are women in the population?[25]

Lotte Hansen: Ah … there are some people nodding their heads now, and it was in a way also kind of what you asked about. Why it was really so funny at all, and why it was important, and I just thought that I … I thought … that I would cut it short and ask if you thought it was important, and you did, and you weren't allowed to answer why, and now I think that people would really like to know why, so now we'll have to take that round briefly. And this has to be a little brief

25 In a survey study of Danish campaigns for increasing female representation in politics, Anette Borchhorst distinguishes between four types of argument: 1) The argument of *interest*. Men and women are considered to have different interests and therefore cannot represent each other politically. The argument, which has its roots in the 1970s' women's movement and socialism, is rarely used by feminist organizations today. 2) The argument of *resource*. Men and women are considered complementary, in that women can contribute with different perspectives, ideas, and solutions from those offered by men. The argument, which has its roots in utilitarianism, is grounded in economic thinking and primarily used by liberalistic politicians. 3) The argument of *justice*. There is no essential difference between men and women. The argument is grounded in ideas of group-based rights and representation in political systems. 4) The argument of *citizenship*, which is related to the argument of justice, is idealistic and has a focus on duties rather than on rights. Borchhorst, "27 procent kvinder i dansk lokalpolitik." In her question, the citizen raises the fundamental issue of available arguments, or topoi, for the campaign. Her own question encourages the debaters to provide arguments *besides* the argument of justice.

because … ah … time is passing. So why should women or those who know some women run for election, if you were to give them a piece of advice?

Citizen: And why should we vote for them? Why should we vote for a woman … rather than a man?

Lotte Hansen: Well, you have to answer this too. Three minutes.

Jette Jensen Clay: Oh well, but I don't want to decide what you should vote for. That's your democratic right, to vote for who you want. But when I say that it is important to have more women in the city council, and when I actually think that the city council ought to be made up of 50 percent women, it is because women make up half of the population in Aarhus, and I don't think that men and women think alike, and then it pisses me off that the men are always making the decisions on my behalf. That doesn't mean that I necessarily always agree with all other women.[26]

Lotte Hansen: No. Nice and short.

Rabih Azad-Ahmad:[27] I think, in relation to representation, but … I th- … if you ask me why, I think it could be good for you to run, that is, you see, because I think it is good to be part of the influence on the politics … and for your … futu- … maybe your future children, in relation to your future, in rela-

26 Jette Jensen Clay represents Enhedslisten, a smaller party on the left. Beside the argument of justice, she uses the argument of interest, emphasizing that men and women are not alike.

27 Rabih Azad-Ahmed, the only male in the panel, represents Det Radikale Venstre, a medium-sized party oriented towards the middle-right.

tion to your study, or whatever you do, or in relation to the environment … and there I also think there are some things that … that … that … you perhaps as a women, because of your network and the people you incl- … what's it called … have more … eh … contact with …, maybe also have some things and angles that you can bring to politics which … which … are not necessarily … ah … or … attended to by men. That, of course, doesn't mean that women only speak for men … the women's cause and men only for the men's cause. But I also think that … that … that there are some things that … that … women also, especially mothers, will be able to see which others wouldn't … eh … ah … But something completely different … I really think it is also incredibly important to talk about tension … that will not be talked about so much, you see, but the thing about having a family … also to women … that is, I have three children … and I am a man, and, of course, it doesn't mean so much if you're a woman or a man because leaving your child, whether you're a man or a woman … that … I don't know … if it means … it means the same, I guess, you love your child, of course, whether you're a man or a woman. In this respect, you can also try, yourself, to organize your time differently … now, it is often the case that I don't see my children before they go to bed, but on the other hand … I in fact get up at half past six even though I have to be at work at nine or ten, also to eat breakfast and spend time with them and then drop them off etc. So, you can also … be a little … family also … organize accordingly … and try to spend a little more time with the family this way.

Lotte Hansen: And, so you have, yes …

Anne Mette Villadsen: You ask why … I will say again that I very much agree with you, Jette … that we … ah … make up over half o-of the population, so this should, of course, also be reflected in the city council politics, but … eh … for example, you could make a difference; if you have something you're enthusiastic about, something you think, this I would actually like to make an impact on politically, then you have, in fact p-particularly in local politics, a great opportunity to … to … come forward with your opinions and to have your opinions implemented, also, so you have a good opportunity to affect the political debate … much more than you have in parliament, for instance.[28]

Camilla Fabricius: That too … you are separated into two parts. One is why you have to vote for women generally and why run … What has really struck me … that … is … an … the entire quality of the children's area. I can think … that you … have made incredible improvements of the library area … there is not a single playground. You see that the city hall park is incredibly beautiful … there is not a single playground. You would never build a museum in Germany without playgrounds. If you move around in the urban space in Copenhagen … so … you … so many exciting playgrounds. This, I actually think, is one of the areas where women make a difference, it is in ordinary practice … in ordinary daily life … there … the way we speak of it to each other … solely in the way we deliberate and discuss things, the way we look at daily life … it is, for instance, one of the things … that … that … that I h-have encountered and thought: why is it like that? Why are the children that I am surrounded by … why don't they have these opportunities? It is because calculations of how many citizens live in this particular place forms the basis, and then you have made some circles, instead of thinking, where do

28 Anne Mette Villadsen represents Det Konservative Folkeparti, a medium-sized conservative party that had been in government since 2000. The emphasis on equal representation is grounded in the argument of justice.

the women and their families and their men go to play? Not, where do they live, but what paths do they have? Why, this is the kind of thing that comes into my mind. And then you say … ahm … why vote for women in general? No, it wasn't quite that … but, why run? You should do that because you can make a difference. I am surprised how much influence you have, in fact. And even though the city council meetings are long, and even though I think, how much interest do I really have in Teknik og Miljø [the Committee for Technology and the Environment], it is really interesting because it is exactly there that I can ask questions about playgrounds – not in Børn og Unge [The Committee for Children and Youth] …[29]

Lotte Hansen: Okay …

Camilla Fabricius: … it is in fact not in Teknik …

Lotte Hansen: I think this was a good example. We'll just finish the round quickly.

Dorthe Laustsen: Well … you have to join, as Jette says … because we make up half of the population in the municipality … and then … ah … it is the politics that we are engaged in … it is that which comes really close to … to … us as citizens who live here in the municipality, it is something that affects us, by and large in everyday life. Eh … I have been on the Teknisk udvalg [The Committee for Technology and the Environment] for two sessions … um … I got into the city council because I was probably most interested in the [laughs]

29 Camilla Fabricious represents Socialdemokraterne, a large, center-left-leaning party. Her emphasis on women's specific perspectives is grounded in a complementary view of the sexes. It is not possible to determine whether her argument is based on the premise of interest or on the premise resource.

social area, but couldn't be … ah … some of the committees because I would have been disqualified at the time … so I joined the Teknisk udvalg, and this actually meant that I came to view the city quite differently … ah … and also regard it from the perspective of the families … ah … I … took … eh … the councillor on a walk with … ah … baby carriage around the town in order to make clear to him what it was like … ah … to be … a child in the municipality of Aarhus … when you walk around town … you are … right at the same level as the tailpipes, and how difficult it is to get around with a baby carriage sometimes. This trip we have taken yet again in this session, also … I have grown somewhat older and because of that I made a proposal for a pedestrian action plan. It has now been adopted by Aarhus City Council, and it is about making some more exciting urban space with room for some of the things that Camilla mentions … that you should try to be more active and create more activities in the urban space as well. Also … I believe that this could be one of the things that women sometimes think of differently, you have another focus, ah … and I have been lucky that the men have also listened in this case.[30]

Lotte Hansen: Great … good example, again … playgrounds … pedestrians, yes …

Laura Hay: I think that the reason why it is important to have more women run is that I believe that women are as competent as men, and if we can't recruit among the women, then we simply won't have the most talented local politicians

30 Dorthe Laustsen represents Socialistisk Folkeparti, a medium to large party on the left of the political spectrum. Besides stressing equal representation (the argument of justice), Laustsen focuses on a particular feminine perspective which could be part of both the topos of interest and the topos of resource.

or, it follows, the best decisions … eh … and as the panel has discussed, there is a very short distance from thought to action in the city council, you have a lot of influence … ahm … In this session we have managed t-to distribute 850 million to renovate schools, this means better toilets, we have in this session made sure that siblings can go to the same school, in fact, it is just about seeing the problems … and then within a period of three months or so, something actually happens … it is an enormously satisfying … and very inspiring … thing to work with.[31]

Lotte Hansen: I think … that … it was a really good answer to your question … ah … and then you were also allowed to say that you made a difference, instead of just saying it was hard. Now, I have actually been asked to round off … and this is going to be done in a very democratic fashion by voting. And … what I would like you to do now … [Explains the voting procedures] So, that's what we'll try now … a small … democratic, maybe a little bit masculine … way t-to make … drive a decision … we can't do any more storytelling now, we have been doing storytelling for one-and-a-half hours, and I think it went pretty well … so is anybody ready to cast their vote yet?

Feminine-Styled Politicians

The Aarhus debate case provides ample opportunity to study the use of feminine style. Taken as a whole, the round of answers displays all of the characteristics that have come to define this style. The meeting in itself has the argumentative structure of example, with the politicians

31 Laura Hay represents Venstre, a large liberalist party that had at the time of the debate been in government since 2000. Her emphasis on competence, recruitment, and talent articulates the liberal side of the argument of resource.

sharing their own experience in order for the audience to identify with them: If this woman can do it, so can the women in the audience. The chairperson's focus on the politicians' own stories, on how they overcame the barriers and decided to run for city council, invites storytelling and anecdotal evidence based on experiential learning. The politicians are role models who are allowed to talk about what worked for them rather than to speak politically about the issue of representation and democracy.

Furthermore, the situational setting of a panel debate, which is part of a campaign, adds its signature to the feminine style. It seems to be a constraint on the politicians' choice of arguments that the debate is supposed to contribute to recruiting female politicians. At least, the debate is conducted with little regard for the qualities that constitute debate, such as a confrontation of opposing views, direct refutation, poignant critique, and, often, trenchant language. In fact, the rounds of answers that the politicians largely agree on, the invitation to share personal experience, the insistence on a practical outcome, the tight schedule maintained by the chair, and the sparse audience involvement firmly ensures that no debate evolves. Even when the citizen in the audience points out that they have spent the time discussing practicalities and reproaches them for having avoided debating the core issue, of "why does gender matter in politics?", they continue to perform feminine style – for instance, by marking agreement with what the 'opponents' have stated earlier.

The citizen develops her questions in a series of comments, but in effect they amount to two. The first one fundamentally questions the relevance of the campaign, "What is it that women as such contribute?" The second one differs only slightly; it is related to voting and citizenship, but is centered on the same epistemological doubt of the political significance of gender: "Why should we vote for a woman … rather than a man?" Both of these questions are grounded in the assumption that there must be more and better reasons than mere equal representation: "Where … what is it … why is it important besides the fact … that … 50 percent of us are women in the population?"

In between these two questions, Lotte Hansen summarizes some of the points leading up to the first question, and in doing so she spells out another question about personal motivation to run. Once again, she implies that the answer should have the structure of a piece of advice from an experienced politician to the novice: "So why should women or those who know some women run for politics, if you were to give them a piece of advice?" Lotte Hansen also confirms that she has understood the critique of the way she has structured the debate, and although her immediate reaction is to defend herself by explaining some of her motives, she ends by acknowledging the relevance of this question: "and then you were also allowed to say that you made a difference, instead of just saying that it was hard."

Interestingly, the answers are quite different, and the employment of the features of feminine style is quite uneven. The citizen's request for more qualitative grounds than the principled premise of equal representation, the argument of justice, is implicitly declined by some of the politicians, whereas others support it. Anne Mette Villadsen makes a short statement of the primacy of equality: "we … ah … make up over half o-of the population, so this should, of course, also be reflected in the city council politics," before she goes on to talk about personal motivation in general. Jette Jensen Clay is in accordance with this topos of justice: "when I actually think that the city council ought to be made up of 50 percent women, it is because women make up half of the population in Aarhus." However, her addition indicates a qualitative difference as she argues from the topos of interest: "and I don't think that men and women think alike, and then it pisses me off that the men are always making the decisions on my behalf." Dorthe Laustsen reiterates the argument of justice as she subscribes to the view that equal representation is a reason for more women to run: "because we make up half of the population in the municipality." But the rest of her contribution is devoted to an anecdotal argument about seeing the city from a child's perspective, and she adds, inductively, that this serves as an example of how women sometimes have a different focus.

The sole male in the panel, Rabih Azad-Ahmad, seems to be at a loss for what reason to give for this persuasive campaign. He starts out by suggesting, generally, that there can be different angles, tentatively relating this to motherhood, but backs down by changing the subject: "But I also think that … that … that there are some things that … that … women also, especially mothers, will be able to see which others wouldn't … eh … ah … But something completely different." In the rest of the entry, he refutes, on a more concrete level, that men and women are essentially different: "that is, I have three children … and I am a man, and, of course, it doesn't mean so much if you're a woman or a man because leaving your child, whether you're a man or a woman … that … I don't know … if it means … it means the same, I guess, you love your child, of course, whether you're a man or a woman." It follows from a denial of gender difference that his own performance of feminine characteristics, plentiful in personal examples and references to parental love and nurturing abilities, is not precluded.

Rabih Azad-Ahmad's confusion reveals that the arguments about gender representation balance on a razor's edge. The qualitative reason, that women (in general) view political issues differently from men (in general), is manifestly essentialist and, consequently, vulnerable to critique based on a deconstruction of the sex versus gender dichotomy – as well as postmodern arguments about gender diversity.[32] On the other hand, if the significance of gender in relation to politics is denied, there can be no qualitative answer to why it is important to have more women in politics. What is left is the quantitative argument about representation of the population: the argument of justice.[33]

---

32 Sylvia Pritsch, *Rhetorik des Subjekts. Zur textuellen Konstruktion des Subjekts in feministischen und anderen postmoderne Diskursen* (Bielefeld: transcript verlag, 2008); Charlotte Kroløkke & Karen Foss, "'Sørg hellere for en solid tremmeseng'," *Rhetorica Scandinavica* 42 (2007).

33 The quantitative warrant for equal representation is challenged by Pitkin, who claims that "if representation means presenting a point of view, one spokesman is

Laura Hay's argument is based on the premise of resource. In contrast to the earlier answers, Laura Hay's response is not solely founded on a topos of equality, but is a qualitative as well as a quantitative argument about the recruitment of talent: "I think that the reason why it is important to have more women run is that I believe that women are as competent as men, and if we can't recruit among the women, then we simply won't have the most talented local politicians and, it follows, not the best decisions ..." Notably, the "we" of Laura Hay's discourse is not a "we" of females, but corresponds to a public plural, a community. Calculating public benefit and emphasizing female competence rather than personal experience, this line of reasoning displays none of the traces of the feminine style. But considering the strict avoidance of feminized arguments, it is all the more striking that Hay ends her entry by adding two examples related to primary schools – an issue that traditionally belongs to a feminine sphere.

One politician stands out by employing feminine style extensively. Camilla Fabricius commences with a series of examples of how playgrounds have been neglected in the urban planning of Aarhus, and she develops her ideas inductively up to the general claim that this is a result of a calculation based on data about where people live, contrary to a female approach like her own which would consider the behavior and whereabouts of the families. Whereas some of the other politicians allude rather vaguely to a difference between men and women, Camilla Fabricius spells out that more is at stake than key female issues; the feminine approach affects both thinking and discourse. This argument is performed in a feminine style which has discursive references to traditional female roles – for instance, that of a housewife deliberat-

---

as good as ten." Hanna Pitkin, *The Concept of Representation* (Berkeley: University of California Press, 1967), 84. However, social scientists have argued that a certain critical mass is necessary. According to Kjær it is worth discussing the possible minimum of a critical mass, considering the stagnation in female representation in Danish municipal councils. Ulrik Kjær, "Kvinder i kommunalpolitik – er grænset nået?" *Kvinder, køn og forskning* 10, 1 (2001): 74.

ing everyday problems with the neighbors: "This, I actually think, is one of the areas where women make a difference, it is in ordinary practice … in ordinary daily life … there … the way we speak of it to each other … solely in the way we deliberate and discuss things, the way we look at daily life … it is, for instance, one of the things … that … that … that I h-have encountered and thought: why is it like that?" The friction-free performance of feminine style – the intimate, self-disclosing tone with appeals to motherhood and domesticity, and the arguments based on experience and induction – is somewhat contrasted by her closing observation that the actual influence she achieved on questions about playgrounds is achieved as a member of the Committee for Technology and Environment, not the Committee for Children and Young People.

To summarize the politician's citation of feminine style, all the defining features are in use, but some politicians cite or perform them more than others. One feature seems to have particular significance in the Danish discourse: frequent references to key political issues related to motherhood and education, such as playgrounds, pedestrian action plans, and the renovation of school toilets. Blankenship and Robson have already emphasized the importance of women's issues in the conceptual development of feminine style. Campbell has also noted the historical importance of special female causes, such as charity, health, and education.

The emphasis on feminine causes is enhanced by the way the chairperson, Lotte Hansen, applauds the politicians for citing feminine style: "Great … good example, again … playgrounds … pedestrians, yes …" Her own performance is, as it happens, worth closer examination. The focus on practical matters such as meal times and secretarial assistance adds to the feminine style used. Earlier in the evening, the list brought about some spectacular domestic metaphors alluding to the nurture and upbringing of children. At some point, she refers to the politicians' preparation of input as "homework", at another she calls the list of suggestions a "pizza menu". Wrapping up before the vote, however, she displays the most telling example: "So, that's what we'll try now … a small … democratic, maybe a little bit masculine … way t-to make … drive a decision … we can't do anymore storytelling now, we have been doing storytelling for one-and-a-half hours, and I think it went pretty well … so is anybody already ready to cast their vote?" Here, she alludes to a suggestion made earlier in the debate by one of the politicians to use storytelling in order to appeal to women, but now it is explicitly opposed to voting as a male, democratic strategy.[34]

Conclusion

According to the official website for Aarhus, female representation in the city council increased by 50 percent in the elections of 2009. Although this was an improvement, women were still under-represented by 39 percent.[35] The result, however, does not allow for a conclusion about the debate's impact on the result. Nor is it possible to measure the actual share of the debaters' feminine style on the increase of female representation.

What may be concluded, however, is that when feminine style was performed, it was clearly performed with a purpose. Some of the politicians' enactment of feminine style aimed at creating identification with an audience of women who could perceive of themselves as valuable political voices. Some of the rhetorical strategies even attempted to legitimize a female perspective as a stronger alterna-

34 The chairperson's relaxed attitude towards the issue of gendered politics could perhaps be viewed as an example of the playful remixing of gender-coded behavior that has been identified as a characteristic of third-wave feminism. See Kroløkke & Foss, "Sørg hellere for en solid tremmeseng." However, the subtle marks of irony that would make this interpretation probable are missing. Rather, her performance of feminine style seems to be the result of an adaptation to norms that she cannot take seriously, but does not bother to oppose either.

35 Aarhus Kommune: https://www.aarhus.dk/da/politik/Byraadet/En-plads-i-Aarhus-Byraad/Kvinder-i-byraadet.aspx. In 2013, however, the number of women in the city council decreased from 12 to 10.

tive to habitual thinking and to conventional ways of deliberating. Still, while acknowledging the debaters' intentions, their actual efforts clearly did not amount to the epistemic or transformative force that was envisioned by some rhetorical critics.

Then what was the problem? Why was the performance of the feminine style not an apt choice in a political campaign in Denmark in 2009? One way to try to answer this question would be to contrast the debaters' rhetorical efforts with Gyrithe Lemche's. In Lemche's speech, the different features of the feminine style – the domestic metaphors, the motherly role of the rhetor, the inductive argument drawing on everyday practice shared by speaker and audience – corresponded to the experiences of the women in the audience. Meanwhile, this basic identification was established for a purpose: to redefine existing identity constructions as essential to a political argument for the women's rights cause.

In judging the rhetorical expediency and political effect of the feminine style, the two following questions seem to be central. 1) Does the feminine style correspond to the acknowledged experiences of the audience? If this identification is established, then 2) Does the rhetoric offer the subjects in the audience a new comprehensive narrative that merges their identification with a political cause?

In the debate in Aarhus City Hall, it is quite obvious that at least some of debaters aim to establish a community of females based on mutual everyday experiences, and on feelings, hopes, and concerns that Danish women share: a busy working life in which time is short. Undoubtedly, the discussion about the logistic difficulties of combining council meetings with a family life would have some resonance for an audience of Danish women. But having established this initial identification, something goes wrong. Where a new identity position could have been reinterpreted and inserted in a grand narrative of, for instance, democratic participation, citizenship, or feminism, the debate fails to meet these aspirations. Addressing the subjects in the audience as young women interested in children's issues in particular, the feminine style of this debate gives the women agency to engage in only a few – traditionally exclusively feminine – areas of society and politics.[36]

It is evident that the performance of feminine style – involving argumentative, stylistic, and narrative choices – reproduces a way of acting and speaking that women have employed for historical and cultural reasons. As a modern rhetorical strategy, a feminine style that perpetually alludes to children is bound to be reductive in comparison with the problems and exigencies that Danish women, politically engaged or not, actually face. In a rhetorical situation where equality is missing, yet seems only barely missed, the local politicians' citation of feminine style cannot be characterized as an apt rhetorical choice. Even though their intentions may have been good, the politicians' performance of feminine rhetoric proves to be a somewhat flawed strategy. It offers only limited rhetorical agency to the women who could potentially become politicians, and as such, the identity position constituted by feminine style is unfortunate. Compared with the ideals of citizenship and democratic deliberation, feminine style equips the female politicians with only some of the arguments, appeals, and devices that are considered as expedient rhetoric.[37]

36 According to Borchhorst's typology of four arguments, my interpretation is grounded in an argument of citizenship which implies the duty of democratic participation.

37 I reached a similar conclusion in an analysis of a leaflet which was part of the general campaign launched by the Ministry for Gender Equality; see Lund, "Retorisk stil." In contrast to the debate, the leaflet employed feminine style as a collective strategy.

CHAPTER FIVE

PROVOCATIVE STYLE

In August 2006, Jostein Gaarder, the bestselling Norwegian author of the popular philosophical book *Sophie's World*, published an article in the Norwegian newspaper *Aftenposten*. It was a direct response to Israel's bombing of south Lebanon, containing a harsh critique of the state of Israel.[1]

The article opens with a denunciation: "Israel is now history. We no longer recognize the State of Israel." The main argument is that the state of Israel seems to act as if it had a divine and historical mandate for its actions. Gaarder attacks this notion from the perspective of a discursively constructed collective identity, a "we" who supposedly are more humanistic and rationalistic than the government of Israel:

> We don't believe in the notion of God's Chosen People. We laugh at this people's capriciousness and weep at its misdeeds. To act as God's Chosen People is not only stupid and arrogant, but a crime against humanity. We call it racism. There are limits to our patience, and there are limits to our tolerance. We do not believe in divine promises as a justification for occupation and apartheid. We have left the Middle Ages behind. We laugh uneasily at those who still believe that the

1 Gaarder, Jostein. "Guds utvalgte Folk," *Aftenposten*, August 5, 2006. An English translation, found on the Simon Wiesenthal Center homepage, is used here. http://www.wiesenthal.com/site/apps/nlnet/content2.aspx?c=lsKWLbPJLnF&b=4442247&ct=5850849.

> god of flora, fauna and the galaxies has selected one people in particular as his favorite and given it silly stone tablets, burning bushes and a license to kill. We call baby killers "baby killers" and will never accept that people such as these have a divine or historic mandate excusing their outrages.

Gaarder is careful to distinguish between the Israeli government and the civilian population; his critique is aimed solely at the state: "May the world therefore have mercy upon the civilian population; for our prophecies of doom are not aimed at the civilian individuals. We wish the people of Israel well, nothing but wellness, but we reserve the right to not eat Jaffa oranges as long as they are foul-tasting and poisonous." Yet, he soon undermines the distinction, painting a vivid picture of hate-driven Israeli children supporting the war: "We ask ourselves if most Israelis think that one Israeli life is worth more than the forty Palestinian or Lebanese lives. For we've seen pictures of little Israeli girls writing hateful greetings on the bombs about to be dropped on the civilian populations of Lebanon and Palestine. The little Israeli girls are not cute when they burst with glee at the death and torment on the other side of the front."

Gaarder's criticism of the "rhetoric of the State of Israel" is structured as a confrontation between an ancient doctrine of vengeful Judaism and the more humanistic stance of Christianity:

> We do not recognize the spiral of retribution and blood vengeance that comes with 'an eye for an eye and a tooth for a tooth.' [...] Two thousand years have passed since a Jewish rabbi criticized the ancient doctrine of 'an eye for an eye and a tooth for a tooth.' He said: 'Do unto others as you would have them do unto you.'

The humanism of the "we" is demonstrated discursively once again in the conclusion, where Gaarder elaborates on, and thereby gives *presence* and salience to, his vision that Israel has ceased to exist. His prophecy of doom has come true, and Israelis have become fugitives: "Shoot not at the fugitives. Take not aim at them! They are vulnerable now – like snails without shells. [...] Give the Israeli refugees shelter; give them milk and honey!"

The provocative devices of Gaarder's contribution were consistent, yet simple. Instead of a sound, critical argument against Israel's policies, Gaarder produced a mockery of biblical language. His references to Jewish religious concepts as "silly stone tablets," "burning bushes," and "milk and honey" are obviously offensive to those who identify with them. Laconic, repetitive sentences imitate the prophecies of doom condemning Israel for its sins. In general, the style of Gaarder's article parodies certain parts of the Bible. The effect of this stylistic choice is a line of reasoning that goes beyond a mere refutation of Israel's policies and actions. The stylistic parody functions as refutation by mockery, performing the idea it attacks: the premise that the state of Israel has a divine mandate for its actions. As such, the style argues a point. In the subsequent debate, however, the offense in alluding to religious symbols and biblical language is bracketed from the argumentative purpose, as it is perceived as the ridicule of religious belief and Jewish culture as such.

The Concept of Provocative Style

Everyday debates rarely live up to the ideals of reason and soundness of argumentation. Thus criticism of actual political and cultural debates is often negative. The claim that I am going to make is that provocative style, mordant irony, and caustic sarcasm are not simply violations of deliberative ideals but vital elements of debate, helping to shape *presence*, structure argument, form opinion, and constitute an engaged and reflective audience.

In this chapter, I argue that provocative style in public debate has a function, and that we err if we simply dismiss provocation as unconstructive. To fully understand the dynamics of public debates, we must study them from a relevant perspective and with relevant critical concepts. My formulation of provocative style as a critical concept is an attempt to better understand properties of rhetorical discourse that are often seen, yet rarely appreciated. My critical approach is closely in tune with Gerard Hauser's theory of public deliberation, Ruth Amossy's theory of polemics, and the rhetorical tradition of the invective. On this basis, it presents a critical scrutiny of a debate on Israel and Jews started by the Norwegian writer Jostein Gaarder in 2006.

In developing the concept of provocative style, I more implicitly draw on a body of twentieth-century rhetorical theories that have established the basis for the argumentative and deliberative approach to style. Perelman and Olbrechts-Tyteca have done important work on the function of rhetorical figures in argumentation. Also relevant is their concept of *presence* as a strategic way of constituting salience. According to Perelman and Olbrechts-Tyteca, the very choice to give presence to some elements instead of others implies their importance and pertinence to the discussion and acts directly on our sensibility. Another major influence on my view of provocative style is Jeanne Fahnestock's *Rhetorical Figures in Science*, introduced in chapter two. In this study of how (some) rhetorical figures structure argumentation and reasoning, Fahnestock sees rhetorical figures not as deviations from ordinary language or a superficial layer that can be removed with no real consequence for the argument – rather, rhetorical figures are the creators of thought, argument, and meaning.

Furthermore, my idea of provocative style draws on some of the critical studies, discussed in chapter three, that develop particular styles as a set of rhetorical characteristics. One example is Robert Hariman's study of political style, in which it is taken to be a compilation of rhetorical features: "a coherent repertoire of rhetorical conventions."[2] Similarly, Barry Brummett defines style as elements working together:

---

2 Hariman, *Political Style*, 4.

"Style is a complex system of actions, objects, and behaviors."[3] Perhaps most evident in this respect is Karlyn Kohrs Campbell's elaborate description of the rhetorical characteristics of the feminine style, studied in the previous chapter. The understanding of style as a coherent compendium is, however, far from novel; it is well established in the aesthetic tradition of studying style, for instance, in its application to periods or nations.[4] But the recent studies deviate from an earlier, notably Romantic, identification of style as an essential quality of the artist's personality or the spirit of an epoch. As discussed in detail in chapter three, recent rhetorical critical studies build on an understanding of style as constitutive of argument and performative of identity, as does my own development of provocative style.

In this chapter, I develop provocative style as a critical concept that functions both as a set of particular stylistic devices that interact as an argument and as an interpretative frame. However, provocative style is defined by more than a loose series of formal features. Provocative style is impertinence; it is a deliberate discursive trespassing of some social norm of interaction. I seek to outline how such a phenomenon may be critically approached below.

Adjusting the Norms to Rhetoric and Polemics

There is a tangible difference between idealized norms of public communication and the actual debates that constitute everyday deliberation. From a rhetorical point of view, the norms may be set too high. At least, the American rhetorical critic Gerard Hauser sees negative

3 Brummett, *A Rhetoric of Style*, xi.

4 See the survey of definitions of style in chapter one, as well as Wolfgang G. Müller's more recent definition of period style: "A period style is to be understood as a set of features of expression and artistic form that are characteristic of a particular epoch (age)." Wolfgang G. Müller, "Epochenstil/Zeitstil," in *Rhetorik und Stilistik*, ed. Ulla Fix et al., 1271.

evaluation as the inevitable outcome of measuring everyday debates by the high standards of ideal speech.

In *Vernacular Voices* (1999), Hauser outlines how pessimism and apathy govern our understanding of public deliberation and political processes: "We still outwardly acknowledge the importance of democratic processes but the deliberative characteristics of public discussion […] are under assault."[5] Disillusionment with, and cynicism toward, "the public" and public deliberation are to a large degree the results of an increasingly marketing-based attitude on the part of political parties and the media, reducing political processes to negative campaigning, reliance on focus groups, and opinion polling. According to Hauser, "Commentators, critics, and theorists surveying this scene are thereby led to a single and compelling conclusion: 'the public' is moribund."[6] Hauser, however, finds that reports of the imminent demise of the public are exaggerated: "Their distortion comes from looking for 'the public' in the wrong places through conceptual lenses radically out of focus."[7] The premises are wrong, or – extending the optical metaphor – the lenses are adjusted to Habermas' rationalistic theory of public communication, but are out of focus when it comes to what goes on in everyday deliberation.

Hauser finds that one of the most obvious problems in Habermas' theory is the grounding of "the public" in shared interests – the idea that discursive deliberation can be defined as disinterested parties discussing some common good:

> Habermas envisions a universalized public sphere populated by disinterested participants who adhere to rationalistic norms and unitary modes of expression on which they base warranted assent. This idealized vision is at odds with the rhetori-

5 Gerard A. Hauser, *Vernacular Voices. The Rhetoric and Publics and Public Spheres* (Columbia: The University of South Carolina Press, 1999), 24.

6 Ibid., 30.

7 Ibid.

> cal features of discourse as it is practiced in a democracy. The addressed and particularized character of discourse on public problems suggests that rhetorical assumptions are a more consonant alternative to those of ideal speech for assessing the discursive practices of actually existing democracy.[8]

Instead of defining "the public" by shared interests, Hauser introduces a rhetorical model in which "we may define a public as the interdependent members of society who hold different opinions about a mutual problem and who seek to influence its resolution through discourse."[9] Thus a public is an activity, and emphasis should be on the discursive process rather than on concrete political entities or groups. In a rhetorical model, participants need not be disinterested; in fact, personal engagement is a defining feature of persuasion.[10]

While Hauser dismisses certain aspects of Habermas' rationalistic model, he still believes that the assessment of rhetorical discourse and the critical inspection of a public sphere depend on some set of communicative norms. This is to be found in the rhetorical tradition. One obvious difference is that instead of testing the validity of discourse by universal norms, we can make judgments according to local conditions of reasoning applied by stakeholders.[11] Hauser's rhetorical normative framework consists of five criteria (permeable boundaries, activity, contextualized language, believable appearance, tolerance), of which I focus on the two – activity and tolerance – that are relevant to my purpose.

---

8 Ibid., 55.

9 Ibid., 32.

10 "Discourse intent on gaining the assent of those who share the consequences of a public problem inevitably addresses them as particular individuals and groups. We adapt our arguments to our audience's readiness to attend, understand, and respond [...] through such rhetorical concerns as *kairos* (timing) and decorum. These rhetorical characteristics of addressed discourse belie the condition of disinterest." Ibid., 50.

11 Ibid., 76.

The first criterion concerns *activity*, or more precisely, *engagement*. According to Hauser, "mass societies tend to treat audiences as passive; they are asked to purchase and to applaud. Publics, on the other hand, are presumed to have a guiding interest for which they have the potential to become active; they are asked their opinions."[12] I agree that activity and engagement among participants are core features in a rhetorical framework. The other rhetorical norm I adopt from Hauser is *tolerance*. Tolerance stems from the very definition of a public sphere as composed of members of society holding different opinions: "Because civil society is constituted by difference rather than identity, by *diversity* rather than unity, contact with alternative ideas and traditions is inevitable."[13] Tolerance, then, is a fundamental condition of communication when consensus is unlikely. While engagement and tolerance are defining characteristics of public deliberation, as rhetorical norms they might, however, be at odds at a practical level. The exploration of the function of provocative style is concerned with the ways in which offensive and provocative features of style and argument initiate and constitute public deliberation as an engaged and engaging activity.

In his specification of critical points of difference between rhetorically conceived communication and the normative frame proposed by Habermas, Hauser touches upon the problem of style. In Hauser's view, Habermas' criterion of generalizable arguments leading to rational consensus imposes a precondition that contains a judgment about language use or style as acceptable modes of argument.[14] Only certain modes of style, not counting for instance vulgar or flamboyant speech, would qualify as public deliberation. As an alternative to treating the tumult of democracy as defective, Hauser puts forward his rhetorical model that reinstates partisan discourse without an *a priori* assessment of its validity: "It would invoke different standards

---

12 Ibid., 77.

13 Ibid., 79.

14 Ibid., 53.

such as kairos or timing, *to prepon* or propriety, immediacy, and adherence, each of which is sensitive to the specificity of audience and the situated character of addressed discourse."[15]

Very much in accord with Hauser's view is the Israeli discourse analyst Ruth Amossy's study of polemics. She deals with polemical discourse as a legitimate mode and integral part of argumentation. Instead of ostracizing discursive violence from the study of argumentation, as has happened in the normative argumentation theories, she turns to more descriptive French discourse analysis as well as interactional studies in order "to account for the way discourse actually works."[16] Her sketching of a conceptual framework designed to examine polemical discourse as an argumentative practice follows from her conclusion that studies on polemics are promoted only by approaches that do not rely on exclusive obedience to Reason or on ethical ideals of communication.[17]

To Amossy, verbal violence is both an argumentative mode – a structure of strong opposition and confrontation of theses – and a discursive register that is a tone of voice, a way of speaking and arguing. Compared with the concept of provocative style, polemics is a broader category with a more general critical aim. My study of the provocative style investigates with more specificity how style and stylistic features function in particular rhetorical exchanges – how style argues, performs, and structures and forms opinion in concrete contexts.

---

15 Ibid. Similarly, in a case study of the polemical style of AIDS activist Larry Kramer, Erin Rand investigates how crescendos of rage and assertions of truth based on a presumed shared morality enable agency and constitute publics. Erin J. Rand, "An Inflammatory Fag and a Queer Form: Larry Kramer, Polemics, and Rhetorical Agency," *Quarterly Journal of Speech* 94, 3 (2008).

16 Ruth Amossy, "The Function of Polemical Discourse in the Public Sphere," in *The Responsibilities of Rhetoric*, ed. Michelle Smith & Barbara Warnick (Long Grove: Waveland Press, 2010), 54.

17 Ibid., 55.

In general, polemical discourse is characterized by excess, for example by a use of hyperbole and a negligence of nuances. However, Amossy stresses that there are limits to the excesses of polemics as an argumentative and discursive mode: "Polemics has to be regulated in order to be efficient: too brutal a transgression of what can be tolerated would ruin the arguer's chances to be heard. In the social arena, one cannot violate taboos without being sanctioned; an excessively brutal disqualification of an opponent would disqualify the speaker herself."[18]

Like Hauser, Amossy argues that the discrepancy between the condemnation of polemics and the frequency of its use calls for a revision of its evaluation. Polemics testifies to the centrality of conflict in public life, as well as the importance of free expression of antagonist views in a democratic sphere. Amossy believes polemics to be a prerequisite for society itself: "polemics is the only way for adversaries sharing the same (national) space to coexist – to live together while sustaining opposing claims and holding antithetical views. Violence is translated into a communication framework, superseding physical fighting or political repression."[19]

Amossy's assertion that verbal violence has the power to supersede physical violence adds a slightly normative touch to her otherwise descriptive approach. Another possibility – unmentioned by Amossy although it is an argument often heard in the debates concerning public verbal assaults – is that discursive violence leads to physical violence. I shall return to a discussion of the effects of violating decorum later.

Another one of Amossy's claims I shall follow up on immediately. According to her, a critique of polemical discourse underlies argumentation theories and rhetoric from antiquity to the present day: "The ancient Greeks denigrated eristic dialogue [...]. Defined as a battle

18 Ibid., 58.

19 Ibid., 59.

where the other has to be defeated rather than convinced, it was criticized for its contempt for truth and its exclusive focus on winning the argument at any price, be it by using fallacies or inflicting humiliation on the opponent."[20] While this account neglects parts of the rhetorical theories it also excludes a widespread rhetorical praxis. To supplement and correct this view, I turn to studies of the Roman invective.[21] My intention is to dwell on some of the chapters in the history of rhetoric that are often ignored by modern rhetorical scholars.

THE RHETORICAL TRADITION OF INVECTIVE

Rather than a formal genre, the antique rhetorical invective should be defined by its intention. The invective aims at annihilating the public image of a person of importance, and this intention can be practiced in literary as well as rhetorical genres. The aim of the speaker is to exclude the target of the invective from the community on the grounds of his or her actions or moral constitution. The invective thus practices in discourse what in Roman culture was a common administrative measure, *damnation memoria*, the demolition of names in inscriptions.[22]

In terms of structure and argumentation, the invective amounts to more than simply shouting abuse at a victim. It is instead a careful construct that draws on several aspects of the rhetorical system, for instance rhetorical figures such as comparison, metaphor, antithesis, irony, and the pun (on names). The Aristotelian theory of rhetorical

20 Ibid., 53.

21 Thomas Conley describes the last decades of the Roman republic, from about 63 to 43 BC, as "the heyday of invective, a period of unprecedented vitriol and nastiness in public disourse." Thomas Conley, *Toward a Rhetoric of Insult* (Chicago: The University of Chicago Press, 2010), 32.

22 U. Neumann, "Invektive (griech. Ψόγος, psógos; διαβολή, diabolé; lat. vituperatio, oratio, invectivs; engl., frz. invective; ital. invettiva)," in *Historisches Wörterbuch der Rhetorik*, vol. 4, ed. Gert Ueding (Darmstadt: Wissenschaftliche Buchgesellschaft, 1998), 549-550.

genres is also useful to the invention of the invective – especially when the epideictic genre and its standard topics of praise are inverted to become topics of blame. Often, the personal attack will be centered on standard accusations and stereotypes, known to the speaker as well as to the audience. For instance, the victim may be accused of being a slave or of slave origin, foreign (barbaric), a thief or of a family of thieves, a sexual deviant, bankrupt, or of being in appearance, clothing, or behavior a dissenter.[23]

As Conley notes, the topics are not only "common" in the sense that they appear relatively frequently; they are also not limited in their application to a particular individual, but may apply in a variety of cases. He gives as an example Cicero's complaint in the *Second Phillipic*, that Antony had unjustifiably maligned Dolabella, alleging adultery. Yet after Dolabella has gone over to Antony's side, Cicero makes a similar charge in quite similar language against Dolabella.[24]

Contrary to Conley's example, which rests on a charge of too much consistency in different oratorical performances, inconsistency in the same speech may also evince how stardardized the topoi of the invective are. In Demosthenes' speech "On the Crown," he blames Aeschines for his humble origins and upbringing: "I have no difficulty finding things to say about you and your family, but it is difficult to decide where I should start. With your father Tromes, who as slave to Elpias, the schoolteacher in the temple of Theseus, wore heavy fetters and a wooden collar."[25] However, later in the speech, the accusation

23 Ibid., 550. Conley's extensive list of stock topics of the Roman invective includes embarrassing family origin, being unworthy of one's family, physical appearance, eccentricity of dress, gluttony and drunkenness, hypocrisy for appearing virtuous, greed and prodigality, taking bribes, pretentiousness, unacceptable sexual conduct, cowardice in battle, bankruptcy, cruelty, and oratorical ineptitude. Conley, *Toward a Rhetoric of Insult*, 37-38.

24 Ibid, 38-39.

25 Demosthenes, *Speeches 18 and 19*. Transl. Harvey Yunis (Austin: University of Texas Press, 2005), 63.

that Aeschines' father is a slave is abandoned in favor of a denigration of his position as a schoolteacher: "But you, you pretentious and haughty man, compare my lot with that enjoyed by you: as a boy raised in that great poverty, serving at the school alongside your father, you rubbed the ink, wiped the benches, and swept the schoolroom, relegated to the status of a household slave, not that of a freeborn youth."[26]As noted by Harvey Yunis, the translator, the profession of schoolteacher is hardly less inappropriate for the father of a political leader,[27] and this is perhaps the reason why what seems like a glaring inconsistency to a modern audience could be acceptable to a Roman.

In his chapter on principles of insult in the rhetorical tradition, Conley accentuates some of the rhetorical functions of commonplaces, in particular that commonplaces are also "common" in their plausibility and ability to sum up "what everybody knows":

> "Everybody knows" that politicians are greedy and corrupt. "Everybody knows" that the powerful and influential attend wild parties and indulge in bizarre sexual behavior (and we should remind ourselves that the members of Cicero's audience were themselves powerful and influential). "Everybody knows" that people who can't speak coherently are either stupid or putting on an act. And so, even in a situation where a given politician is neither, in fact, corrupt nor putting on an act, it could be true, it "makes sense," "it could happen."[28]

According to Neumann, this reliance on social norms is exactly what defines the invective. The essence of the invective lies in the ability to create an identity of norms between the speaker and the audience; it confirms the valid norms and values by contrasting them to the object

26 Ibid.

27 Ibid., 95.

28 Conley, *Toward a Rhetoric of Insult*, 39.

of the invective *ex negativo*.[29] As a consequence, while the author of the invective seeks to make the adversary appear a social outsider or even an enemy of society, he will style himself as a "vir bonus."

That an agenda this conservative is reached through breaches of social conventions may seem paradoxical. Nevertheless, this is exactly what is at stake: The invective reaches its goals through a deliberative violation of decorum. The inevitable distaste of such conduct is legitimized by claims of necessity – in most invectives of Antiquity, the speaker emphasizes that the personal attack is not natural to him, but is something he is forced to do because of the circumstances.[30]

While the invective was widespread and quite acceptable in Antiquity, it was used to confront groups of enemies such as Jews, heretics, and heathens in early Christianity.[31] In the Middle Ages, new forms that were definitely influenced by the antique tradition appeared. Lampoons and libels occurred in several of the media of the time, such as leaflets, speeches, and especially religious sermons.[32] These new forms witness that although the invective is terminologically tied to Antiquity, its tradition of public personal condemnation goes on. By the Enlightenment, however, polemics influenced by personal attack are no longer considered to be a legitimate kind of controversy. According to the communicative ideals of the age, a good debate is achieved by separating the person from the substance, and the private from the public. In public discourse, debaters strive to obtain a good tone and polite behavior – norms which find their philosophical basis in a united endeavor to reach the truth.[33]

---

29 Neumann, "Invektive," 551.

30 Ibid.

31 Ibid, 555. In Antiquity, there was no real distinction between public and private. Therefore, argumentation *a persona* would not disqualify the argument or the speaker. Hanne Roer & Marie Lund Klujeff, "Introduktion," *Rhetorica Scandinavica* 57 (2011), 9.

32 Neumann, "Invektive," 555.

33 Ibid., 557.

Today, the ideals of the Enlightenment are maintained, in theories of – among other things – argumentation and normative rhetoric. Meanwhile, the practice of libel, fierce polemic and personal attack has not ceased to influence the public debate. As argued by Hauser and Amossy, the discrepancy between theory and practice is an incontestable problem: Today, universal norms for assessing communicative practice only poorly equip the critic to understand (some of) the discourse that makes up public debate. My concept of provocative style attempts to provide the critic with some of the necessary analytical tools to confront, criticize, and understand controversies and debates. With that purpose, I now return to the debate provoked by Jostein Gaarder.

The Jostein Gaarder Debate

As might be imagined, a heated debate followed from Jostein Gaarder's article, on both the printed pages and the website of *Aftenposten.* Soon the debate engaged international participants, some of whom were outraged, some sympathetic. Both positions are represented in the following excerpts from two articles on the debate webpages of *Aftenposten.* The first is an open letter from Dr. Shimon Samuels, the director for international relations at the Simon Wiesenthal Center in Paris. "Jostein Gaarder, the author of the literary chef d'oeuvre, *Sophie's World,* has become seriously ill, either with malice, or, perhaps, Alzheimer's or both. Translated into 53 languages and with 26 million copies sold, so many of his readers will mourn Gaarder's current loss of vision, coherence and, above all, his recruitment to the forces of darkness."[34]

Uwe Wagner, a German citizen from Rostock, supported Gaarder. Unlike the professional spokesperson for the Wiesenthal Center, Wagner built his ethos as a person independent of organizational interests

34 Shimon Samuels: "Wiesenthal Centre's Open Letter to the People of Norway in the Oslo Daily Aftenposten, http://www.wiesenthal.com/site/apps/nlnet/content2.aspx?c=lsKWLbPJLnF&b=4442247&ct=5850849.

but possessing the relevant moral and intellectual qualities. He had fought for a good cause in the past (*areté*), and was therefore rhetorically in a position to insist on a more nuanced debate (*phronesis*):

> In my opinion, Mr. Gaarder is absolutely right. Millions of Jewish people were killed in the past by the German Hitler-fascists. And I myself fought against German fascists [...]. But this mass murder cannot be a justification for the reign of terror the ruling politicians of Israel organize against the Arabian people. It is an infamy to denounce Mr. Gaarder as an anti-Semitic man. The same perfidious methods we know here in Germany: you have criticism against the policy of Israel's leaders, so you are automatically an anti-Semite.[35]

The obvious result of Gaarder's provocative style was the formation of an active public engaged in deliberation. As such, Gaarder's entry kickstarted a debate that was soon taken over by other active participants. While the provocative aspects of Gaarder's style were not disputed explicitly in the examples quoted above, their effects can still be sensed. Samuels responded to the anger and dismay Gaarder's article caused by raising doubts about his sanity. Wagner, on the other hand, reproduced the indignation of Gaarder's article in his defense of the right to criticize the state of Israel without being dismissed as anti-Semitic. Both statements bear the stamp of provocative style. Thus the debaters seem to adopt, by citation or imitation, the provocative style that Gaarder's article introduced.

The provocative style was certainly picked up in a leading article in the *Weekly Standard,* an American magazine, by its right-leaning editor, William Kristol, who opened by evoking the anti-Semitic sentiments of the early twentieth century:

---

35 Uwe Wagner, "Letter to the editor," *Aftenposten*, August 6, 2006. http://www.aftenposten.no/ english/local/article1416800.ece

> "How odd / of God / To choose / The Jews." Thus the British journalist (and communist) William Norman Ewer, in the early part of the last century. The reply came from Cecil Browne: "But not so odd / As those who choose / A Jewish God / But spurn the Jews." Browne's riposte may have won the poetic exchange. But Ewer's anti-Judaism prevailed in the next decades in Europe. Buried there after World War II, hatred of the Jews flourished for the rest of the 20th century in the Middle East. Is anti-Judaism now enjoying a broader revival? It would seem so.[36]

Kristol concluded that "Jews are under attack. And no one seems much concerned" – which is also the title of his article. Four examples backed up his claim, of which Gaarder's article was just one. On Gaarder, Kristol wrote:

> Mr. Gaarder's distaste for Israel seemed to be based on his dislike of Israel's policies, his revulsion against the God of Israel ("an insatiable sadist"), and his anger that, "for two thousand years, we have rehearsed the syllabus of humanism, but Israel does not listen." It's not clear who that "we" has been for two thousand years. But since Israel has only existed since 1948, it is presumably the Jews, not merely Israel, who have not listened. (It was, however, generous of Mr. Gaarder to call for mercy on the Jewish civilian population.)

Although these few lines fail to render an exact account of the content of Gaarder's article, Kristol pinpointed how Gaarder's argument was based on the very premise he defied (the conflation of state and religion). This inconsistency made it easy for Kristol to ignore Gaarder's

36 William Kristol, "Anti-Judaism," *Weekly Standard*, September 11, 2006.

recurring claim that his criticism was aimed not at civilians but at the state of Israel.

The commonsensical reasoning and the mild irony at the end of the paragraph veil the force of Kristol's particular brand of provocative style. Kristol used this piece to launch the conspiracy theory that Jews, in America as well as internationally, historically as well as today, are under attack by the powerful and the cultural elite. The humble style of his refutation of Gaarder seems an attempt to enact the vernacular by speaking in the voice of the victimized. Additionally, Kristol's provocative style is characterized by large claims with little backing, as well as a highly selective reading of Gaarder. Besides the framing of Gaarder's article as part of an international Jew-bashing trend, Kristol takes a specific expression, "an insatiable sadist," out of its exact context. Thereby Kristol disregards the fact that Gaarder, rather than denouncing the Jewish God in general, is discussing a specific tale, arguing that, "in that tale, the Lord God of Israel appears as an insatiable sadist."

To recapitulate the particulars of provocative style, the most obvious feature is its violation of decorum. In its deliberate overstepping of norms of public communication, the provocative style can be identified as a species of the vernacular. It is a nonofficial public discursive practice that is easily combined with a speaking position of the outraged, or even the victimized. Another characteristic of the provocative style is its elaborate stylistic performance of the argument. In the Gaarder example, the mimicking of Jewish concepts and biblical tone functions as a refutation of the idea of a divine mandate. As a consequence, certain biblical topoi are present in the argumentation, and this presence seems to be another significant feature of the provocative style. Furthermore, provocative style tends to be "cited" or copied in the ensuing conversation.

Taken as a whole, the Gaarder-Kristol controversy provided ample evidence of what we may now characterize as provocative style. That the immediate effect was an active public engaging in deliberation is not disputed – but the debate was very far from ideal. While both sides delivered fairly strong and strategic partisan contributions, displaying argumentative and stylistic skills, they also violated some norms of public deliberation. Gaarder's article was weakened by argumentative inconsistency that made it vulnerable to criticism. Kristol's representation of Gaarder's argument was biased and manipulative.

About one week after his initial piece appeared, Gaarder wrote another article entitled "Forsøk på Klargjøring" ("Attempt at Clarification").[37] Studies of apology and atonement have plentifully demonstrated how discrepancies between the speaker's explicit statements of the purpose of the speech and the strategies used govern many apologies.[38] In Gaarder's clarification, he explained how his use of rhetorical devices caused a misunderstanding. He emphasized the emotional context of the original article, quoting the line "not as of this writing, not in the hour of grief and wrath," and explained that it was written the same day that pictures from Qana came in. Using differentiation as a strategy, he sought to separate the stylistic and emotional aspects of the article from "the real message," and claimed that he never meant to say that Jewish religion and culture were inferior to the humanism found in Christian and Muslim history. The criticism was aimed solely at the notion of "God's chosen people," which, he said, he still understood as a divine mandate for political action.

By using differentiation strategies, Gaarder minimized the importance of his style while defending his argument. Whether as a strategy of defense or as a theory of signs, this separation of style and argument (form and meaning) is not warranted by modern theories of metaphor, rhetoric, and style. The constitutive and argumentative function of style and rhetorical figures has been established in numerous studies, including those mentioned above. As for the specific case, Gaarder's attempt to separate stylistic and literary devices from the "real argu-

37 Jostein Gaarder, "Forsøk på Klargjøring," *Aftenposten*, August 12, 2006. http://www.aftenposten.no/meninger/kronikk/Forsok-pa-klargjoring-393867b.html.

38 See for instance, Joy Koesten & Robert C. Rowland, "The Rhetoric of Atonement," *Western Journal of Communication* 55 (2004); Lisa S. Villadsen, "Speaking on Behalf of Others," *Rhetoric Society Quarterly* 38 (2008).

ment" is misplaced. His criticism of the idea that a certain group of people should have a divine mandate to act politically is argued forcefully in the stylistic parody employed in his initial article. The style was provocative, but as such it functioned as a line of argument that Gaarder stood by in his clarification.

Although Gaarder's article provoked both offense and irritation, it also gave rhetorical salience to a conflict that Scandinavian audiences often see as "Other." It functioned as an argumentative selection of data giving *presence* to the complex problems of Israeli history, politics, and religion. Temporarily isolating the conflict from abstract world politics, Gaarder's style reclaimed its relevance for an audience responsive to allusions to "milk and honey," familiar to them from their childhood narratives. During the debate, opinions were formed ("a criticism of the State of Israel is not identical to fascism"; "Jews are under attack"). In this respect, the debate did constitute an audience and engage it in rhetorical citizenship, forming and stating opinions in order to seek influence. In assessing the specific case, I believe that its importance was far from neutralized by the offenses and attacks perpetrated by the debaters.

Critical Reflections

Having identified the features and functions of provocative style, and assessed its qualities, the problem of conflicting norms prevails: How are rhetorical critics to balance those incommensurable values – an engaged public and communication ethics – on a more general level? Returning to Hauser, we find that although interests and partisan appeals are acceptable to him, he by no means subscribes to a philosophy of 'anything goes.' Rather, it is essential to the norms of a rhetorical model that they "offer encouragement toward the achievement of a common mind rather than advancement of vested interests."[39] Hauser,

---

39 Hauser, *Vernacular Voices*, 80.

like Perelman and Olbrechts-Tyteca, draws the line at propaganda, distinguishing between "partisan urgings, in which responsiveness to the other side and the possibility of being persuaded are assumed, and the manipulation of propaganda."[40]

A similar caution and concern for the constitutive aspects of pernicious discursive practices is found in James A. Mackin's study of a much earlier sample of oratory, Pericles' funeral oration. Mackin reasons in terms of an environmental metaphor as he considers "a social system as an ecosystem that goes beyond the physical to incorporate the symbolic."[41] He traces how Pericles' oration damaged the Athenian community as an ecosystem through a process of "symmetrical schismogenesis," a progressive differentiation that resulted in polarization. In rhetorical stylistic terms, he shows how the use of antithesis to intensify partisanship at one level of the social system necessarily results in a tearing apart of community at another level. Pericles' antithesis emphasizes the antagonism between Athens and Sparta, at the same time that it artistically creates consubstantiality and strengthens the Athenian sense of community. Yet by reinforcing Athenian uniqueness and describing Athens as a closed ecosystem, Pericles undermined the larger communicative ecosystem of the Greek city-states. Mackin's concern is the long-term effect of this kind of rhetorical pollution of an ecosystem: "The rhetorical chasm that Pericles created by his artful use of antithesis may well have contributed to the ultimate decline of Athens."[42]

One critic who is engaged in describing and appreciating the function of vitriol in a democracy is Amossy. In correspondence with her appreciative approach, she believes that polemical discourse is governed by a strategic principle that will, in the end, prevent too harsh an overstepping of public norms. From her perspective, the

---

40 Ibid.

41 James A. Mackin Jr., "Schismogenesis and Community: Pericles' Funeral Oration," *Quarterly Journal of Speech* 77, 3 (1991): 251.

42 Ibid., 256.

tastelessness of personal attack disqualifies the speaker in the eyes of a contemporary public, and consequently makes it an ineffective rhetorical argument.[43] In addition, Amossy's theory is based on the premise that abusive discursive attacks have the function of precautionary measures against physical violence. A similar topos of substitution is intrinsic to Neumann's definition of the invective. According to Neumann, the ancient invective was a discursive counterpart to the physical eradication of names in inscriptions.

My own stand in the discussion of legitimacy as efficacy would be a step further to the cautious side. I am not completely confident that a logic of self-regulation can be trusted to perform the function of last bastion before the ultimately distorted public sphere. History should have taught us that norms of societies may change for the worse. What in my view seems crucial is neither to glorify, nor demonize provocations, personal attacks, or verbal aggressions. Instead of assessing them from an agenda of praise or blame, they should be dealt with analytically and critically. A very first step must be to study public debates, closely and on their own terms. I have put forward "provocative style" as a critical concept in order to enable rhetorical critics to perceive what has sometimes been overlooked in the study of public deliberation. In this way I propose that increased understanding is sustained by careful rhetorical analysis and cautious interpretation, not by assuming the worst (or best).

Consequently, I hope that the concept of provocative style will be able to counterbalance suggestions of vast and potentially irreparable damage grounded in critical topoi such as 'fear of the precedent' and 'unlimited development.'[44] As a critical tool, provocative style aims to enable the critic to scrutinize debates and debate cultures on a more concrete level. Furthermore, it is intended to encourage the rhetorical critic to examine and reflect on the possible functions of a

43 Ibid.

44 Perelman & Olbrechts-Tyteca, *The New Rhetoric*, 181-192.

heated debate: Does the verbal aggression have a purpose? Can it be interpreted as a critique of power?[45] Is the crux of the matter political (although it seems to be of a personal nature)?[46] When viewed in a gentler light, fierce polemics and personal attacks may appear purposeful and rhetorically powerful. The conceptualization of provocative style insists on a bracketing into stages and elements. There are engaging factors, argumentative functions, and argumentative faults, all of which should be studied and appreciated before they become part of a critical evaluation.

45 Annie Mattsson, "Den tyranniske teaterkungen. Smædelser mot Gustaf III," *Rhetorica Scandinavica* 57 (2011).

46 Christina Holst Færch, "En særdeles parfumeret retorik. Smædeversets retorik og politisk dyd i 1700-tallets Danmark," *Rhetorica Scandinavica* 57 (2011).

CHAPTER SIX

SPEECHWRITING AND STYLE

The first speaker at an annual speechwriting seminar arranged by the rhetorical consultant firm *Rhetor* in November 2012 was the Danish Member of Parliament and former minister Bertel Haarder. Although he was known for writing his own speeches rather than using ones written by government office speechwriters, he provided an apt metaphor for logography: "The speech must be tailored to the speaker: it must be customized to fit the waist measurement and the length of the legs." During the seminar, other participants returned to the metaphor that established a similarity between speeches and clothing. Meanwhile, there was another recurring topos for speechwriting: that the speech must reflect the personality of the speaker.

In a practical sense, both topoi refer to the need for the speechwriter to obtain knowledge of the speaker's general frame of reference, to get to know her opinions, experiences, taste, upbringing, family background, and so on. But they also allude to language and style. The two ways of speaking about speechwriting – as an item of clothing or as an expression of the speaker's personality – should be familiar topoi by now. They are, as I have argued in previous chapters, tenacious perceptions of style in Western culture. In this last chapter, I will probe the thesis that Müller's theory about the two dominant topoi of style may be transplanted to rhetorical theory about logography, the practice of writing speeches for others.

In the following pages, I shall look for the two topoi in the somewhat unsystematic rhetorical theory of speechwriting. I compare contemporary rhetorical theories of speechwriting and style with ancient sources that focus on the concept of dramatic character: *ethopoeia*. The investigation has two perspectives; in the first, the speech is viewed as a tailored garment made to fit the speaker, while in the other, the speech is thought to express the individuality and personality of the speaker. The latter especially seems to be dominant in the practice and theory of contemporary speechwriting. I argue that a third perspective, allowing for a more dynamic and constitutive perception of speechwriting, is needed. To conclude, I discuss two prevalent stylistic ideals in speechwriting: the eloquent style and the conversational style.

Who is Speaking?

In the article "Ghostwriting and the Rhetorical Critic" (1960), Ernest G. Bormann studies how the increasing use of professional speechwriters affects rhetorical criticism of speeches. When the rhetorical critic studies biographical details in order to understand the ideas in the speech, the aspect of ghostwriting becomes relevant: "The delivery of the speech is influenced by the speaker's preparation and it is within the analysis of speech preparation that the most careful research is required when ghostwriters are discovered."[1] Bormann refers to an analysis of Franklin D. Roosevelt's preparation of speeches which shows that several persons contributed with formulations and ideas. The problem with speechwriting is that the speaking person becomes blurred: "Was the 'quarantine' expression in Roosevelt's address of October 5, 1937, actually Roosevelt's, or Rosenman's, or Ickes'?"[2]

The speaker's style, the most personal aspect of speechwriting, is also the aspect which is influenced the most by the inference of a

1 Ernest G. Bormann, "Ghostwriting and the Rhetorical Critic," *Quarterly Journal of Speech* 46, 3 (1960): 284-288.

2 Ibid, 285.

speechwriter. Bormann quotes Marie Hochmuth Nichols, who assumes that the style of a speech tells the critic something about the speaker's personality and his attitude towards the audience: "If style is the man himself, then a close scrutiny of the details of style should tell us what manner of man is doing the speaking and in what relationship he conceives himself to be with his audience."[3] In comparison, Bormann seems to be less concerned with the speaker's relationship with the audience and more with the representation of the speaker's personality: "The ghostwriter understands the importance of using a style that is appropriate to the speaker. He makes every effort to adapt his language to the personality of his client."[4]

Bormann distinguishes between two schools of rhetorical criticism. The first is named "speaker-oriented rhetorical criticism," a biographical oriented critique that values textual authenticity highly. The other, characterized as "speech-oriented criticism," is a formalistic criticism that draws on the principles of art criticism. However, Bormann hesitates to apply speech-oriented criticism to *ghostwriting*:

> the ghostwriter makes the artistic criticism of speeches difficult if not impossible, because there is very little that is artistically worth studying in his efforts. The reason for this is that the ghost, writing for someone else, tends not to write as well as he can. The ghost has a tendency to be discreet and careful. He weakens adjectives and tones down the strength of statements. He knows the punishment for a misstatement or a careless word. He weighs and ponders every expression, and as a result, he dilutes the distinctiveness and strength and spontaneity of whatever writing talent he may have.[5]

---

3 Ibid. Marie Hochmuth, "The Criticism of Rhetoric," in *A History and Criticism of American Public Address* vol. 3, ed. Marie Hochmuth (New York: McGraw-Hill, 1955).

4 Bormann, "Ghostwriting", 286.

5 Ibid., 287.

The bad influence of speechwriting is even more distinct when speeches are written by a group of speechwriters: "What emerges from this process, no matter how talented the individual writers are, is a sort of grammatically correct, innocuous prose, not well suited for artistic criticism. [...] Style may be the man, but when that style is five men, it ceases to be any style at all."[6]

Bormann concludes that the widespread use of professional speechwriters in American politics is harmful to both the democratic public debate and rhetorical criticism:

> As the public becomes more and more cynical about the authorship of speeches, the ethos of the speaker is undermined; the speech loses its hold upon the public as a vital factor in public affairs. The level of rhetoric declines and its function as a fundamental tool of the winnowing of ideas in a democratic society is lost. With this decline, the justification for rhetorical criticism declines as well.[7]

The Ethics of Speechwriting

With this conclusion, Bormann strikes on the ethical theme which becomes the object of scrutiny in "The Ethics of Ghostwritten Speeches" (1961), written the following year.[8] In this article, he suggests that the

6 Ibid., 288.

7 Ibid. Marie Hochmuth Nichols expresses a similar concern for the ethical and qualitative consequences that speechwriting may have on public speech. Marie Hochmuth Nichols, *Rhetoric and Criticism* (Baton Rouge: Louisiana State University Press, 1972).

8 Ernest G. Bormann, "Ethics of Ghostwritten Speeches," *Quarterly Journal of Speech* 47, 3 (1961), 262-267. Lois L. Einhorn observes how Bormann's term *ghostwriting* is immanently a negative judgment, whereas most critics since then have used the concepts "ghostwriter" and "speechwriter" as interchangeable terms. Another, more neutral definition of *ghostwriter* would be: "one who surreptitiously prepares written and oral messages for public figures below the highest levels." Lois

borrowing in speechwriting should be viewed as an ethical continuum; at one end we find acceptable advice, for instance from a spouse, and in the other professional, strategic speechwriting which is a deceit. Repeatedly, he accentuates that authenticity in the representation of the speaker's personality is crucial to the judgment of the ethics of the speech:

> If the audience is to know a candidate through what he speaks and writes, then he must be honest with them and present himself as he really is. When he reads a speech that reveals to his audience a quiet humor, an urbane worldliness, subtle and incisive intellectual equipment, then he should be that kind of man. If his collaborators, one a man of quiet humor, another an urbane worldly man, and the third a man of subtle and incisive intellectual equipment, are responsible for the "image" revealed in the speech, and if the speaker has different qualities and intellectual fiber, the speech is a deceit and it can be labeled as ghostwritten and condemned as unethical.[9]

In relation to Bormann's distinction between two schools of rhetorical criticism, his own position is in the speaker-oriented school. The origins of the speech are essential to this critical position, which focuses on the speaker's biography and the creative process. Within this paradigm of thought, ethical problems arise because the speech pretends to be written by someone other than the person who has actually written it.

The other critical approach, the speech-oriented school, is dismissed by Bormann's because of its attachment to artistic criticism. However, from a contemporary perspective, the value of Bormann's distinction between two schools of criticism seems not so much to lie in the discussion of artistry in speechwriting, as in the opposition

---

J. Einhorn, "The Ghosts Unmasked: A Review of Literature on Speechwriting," *Communication Quarterly* 30, 1 (1982): 43.

9 Bormann, "Ethics of Ghostwritten Speeches," 267.

of a Neo-Aristotelian criticism oriented towards biography versus a text-oriented close analysis of the speech.[10] Thus, the latter – with its discursive focus on, for instance, argumentative and stylistic structures – offers a way out of the ethical problem of 'whose ideas' it is. I shall return to this discussion later.

Although Martin J. Medhurst diverts the discussion off the ethical route, he maintains the interest in the author and the author's influence on the genesis of the speech. He directs attention to a series of other aspects that are major influences on speechwriting. For instance, he argues that the widespread use of speechwriters affects the analysis of the speaker's inventional resources: "It is a choice not about ideas or arguments, but about people."[11]

According to Medhurst, the problem of authorship is not solved by turning it into a matter of ethics:

> Recognizing that the true authorship of presidential addresses is often hidden from public inspection, we reasoned that the president was nevertheless *responsible* for the speech as delivered. We "solved" the problem of authorship by transforming it into a well-meaning concern about ethics. [...] Important as these questions are, they nevertheless fail to address the basic problem of authorship and its implications for the process of rhetorical invention.[12]

The point is further elaborated in the book *Presidential Speechwriting* (2003). In its introduction, Medhurst debunks the myth that the

10 "Neo-Aristotelian rhetorical analysis typically includes a biographical sketch of the speaker, considering the individual's education, speech training, and other factors that could influence ideas and style." Einhorn, "The Ghosts Unmasked," 44.

11 Martin J. Medhurst, "Ghostwritten Speeches: Ethics isn't the only Lesson," *Communication Education* 36 (1987), 241.

12 Ibid., 241.

American public would be better off if presidents wrote their own speeches and expressed their own opinions and ideas:

> As appealing as this line of reasoning may be, it is, I believe, fundamentally mistaken – for several reasons. First, presidents represent the nation, not merely themselves. They speak on behalf of the people and represent the views of the nation as refracted through the lenses of party, ideology, political and economic constraints, and situational variables. They do not – and cannot – simply state their own personal views. They need good advisors and speechwriters precisely for this reason – so that their discourse represents the best articulation of policy or position possible.[13]

Even though Medhurst both highlights the benefits of speechwriting and draws attention to critical aspects other than the ethical, he adheres to a logic of influence central to Bormann's speech-oriented school. But the study of style in speechwriting is not exclusively linked to the preparation of the speech; rather, style has proved to be a constant presence in the rhetorical criticism of speechwriting.

---

13 Martin J. Medhurst: "Introduction. Presidential Speechwriting: Ten Myths That Plague Modern Scholarship," in *Presidential Speechwriting. From the New Deal to the Reagan Revolution and Beyond*, ed. Kurt Ritter & Martin J. Medhurst (College Station: Texas A & M University Press, 2003), 10. Other rhetorical critics have investigated the functional rather than ethical implications of professional speechwriting, for instance Jaap de Jong and Bas Andesweg, who have developed a method which combines quantitative analysis, qualitative interviews, and rhetorical criticism. See Jaap de Jong & Bas Andesweg, "All's Well that Ends Well: The Problem of Peroratio in Ministerial Speeches," in *Rhetorical Aspects of Discourse in Present-Day Society*, ed. Lotte Dam, Lise-Lotte Holmgreen, & Jeanne Strunck (Newcastle: Cambridge Scholars Publishing, 2008); Jaap de Jong an&d Bas Andesweg, "Professionalizing Speech Production. Changes in 15 Years of Ministerial Speeches," in *Bending Opinion: Essays on Persuasion in the Public Domain*, ed. Ton van Haaften et al. (Leiden: Leiden University Press, 2012).

The Style of the Speaker

As it appears from the discussion among American critics summarized above, the speaker's style and language are recurrent motives in rhetorical criticism on speechwriting. According to Lois J. Einhorn, style is one of the most important questions for the theory of speechwriting. She suggests a change of the old maxim 'style is the man' to "style is the ghost's interpretation of the man."[14] Evidently, Einhorn implies a reinterpretation of Comte de Buffon's saying "Le style est l'homme même." Similar allusions to Buffon are made above by Hochmuth Nichols ("If style is the man himself, then a close scrutiny of the details of style should tell us what manner of man is doing the speaking") and Bormann ("Style may be the man, but when that style is five men, it ceases to be any style at all").[15] In addition, the idea is central to the ethical imperative that the speech should be an authentic expression of the speaker's personality – it must represent the speaker 'as he really is.'

The way that style is conceptualized in rhetorical criticism on speechwriting perfectly matches Müller's theory about the two topoi that have dominated the thinking on style from Antiquity until today. As recounted in the previous chapters, one topos views style as the dress of thought while the other assumes an identity between style and the speaker's personality. In my opening anecdote, the Danish minister Bertel Haarder compared the speech to tailored clothing – a clear-cut example of the first. The discussion between American rhetorical critics above is founded on the other topos.

---

14 Einhorn, "The Ghosts Unmasked," 45.

15 In a chapter about "Ghost Writing" in a later book, Nichols emphatically dissociates herself from the idea that style gives access to the speakers true self – at least when speechwriters are involved in the writing process: "Eric Sevareid's notion that 'a man's own words are a man's own self,' which has been our assumption, too, in doing rhetorical criticism, takes on an antique air [...]. We have long been aware that criticism is crippled in dealing with style. Attributing characteristics of style to a speaker who has a host of ghost writers around is risky." Hochmuth Nichols, *Rhetoric and Criticism*, 44-45.

As noted earlier, Müller seems to have erred in his assumption that the consolidation of the Romantic topos 'style as the incarnation of the poet's soul' led to the extinction of the competing topos. At least when speechwriting is concerned, it is quite easy to find examples of the analogy of style as dress of thought. For instance, the Danish rhetorical critic Merete Onsberg provides a rather elaborate example: "A speech cannot be cut like ready-to-wear clothing; measurements must be taken, and it must be adjusted to the one who has to 'wear the clothes.'"[16] She substantiates her argument with the successful working relationship between President John F. Kennedy and his speechwriter Theodore C. Sorensen:

> In this collaboration which developed over a decade, they created, without really being aware of it, Kennedy's speaking style. It was not a style that Kennedy spoke in private, but in public: "I believe in human dignity as the source of national purpose, in human liberty as the source of national action, in the human heart as the source of national compassion and in the human mind as the source of our invention and our ideas ..." Thus spoke Kennedy in a speech in 1960 to the Liberal Party in New York. Sorensen continues: "He said this and he believed it. But he had not written it and did not naturally speak of his philosophical outlook in such grandiloquent terms."[17]

It is worth noticing that when the topos is used in relation to speechwriting, the simile not only constitutes a likeness between style and a garb – with the connotations that language is something added, that it has aesthetic and social functions, and that it should fit an otherwise

16 Merete Onsberg, "En mand er en mand, og et ord er et ord – men hvis ord er mandens? Om nogle retoriske problemer ved den politiske taleskrivning," *Retorikstudier* 11 (1998), 36. My translation.

17 Ibid. My translation. Theodore C. Sorensen, *Kennedy* (London: Hodder and Stoughton, 1965), 22.

unchanged substance. Both Bertel Haarder and Merete Onsberg twist the metaphor further and insist that the dress be tailor-made; it must match the speaker's individuality.

However, a close reading of Onsberg's example of Sorensen and Kennedy's cooperation shows that it is actually not a very precise illustration of the dress metaphor. On the contrary, Sorensen emphasizes that the style of the speech is neither representative of Kennedy's personality, nor customized to it. If anything, Onsberg's interpretation of the example seems to indicate that in speechwriting something entirely new is created: "In this collaboration which developed over a decade, they created, without really being aware of it, Kennedy's speaking style."

Kennedy's particular speaking style has also been the object of a study conducted by Kathleen Hall Jamieson, although she evaluates it in quite another light. Indeed, to her, the marked contrast between Kennedy's private and public speaking styles is a weak point: "A person familiar only with Kennedy's public speech would be hard pressed to guess that the following remarks were made by the president who asked 'not what your country can do for you.'" [18] Jamieson refers to some remarks uttered by Kennedy in private about a conflict with American steel workers: "And they kicked us right in the balls. And we kicked back. The question really is: are we supposed to sit there and take a cold, deliberate fucking?"[19] Jamieson posits President Ronald Reagan, who spoke with more consistency, as Kennedy's rhetorical opposite.

Reagan appeared to be the same person whether he was speaking in public from a manuscript or in a less formal situation.

More recently, American rhetorical critic Kristine S. Bruss has examined rhetorical style in relation to the composition of the speaker's

18 Kathleen Hall Jamieson, *Eloquence in an Electronic Age. The Transformation of Political Speechmaking* (Oxford: Oxford University Press, 1988), 177.

19 Ibid. Benjamin C. Bradlee, *Conversations with Kennedy* (New York: W.W. Norton, 1975).

character. To this end, she compares contemporary logography with ancient rhetorical theories on *ethopoeia*. The basis of her investigation of contemporary practices is the experienced speechwriter for business leaders, Alan Perlman, who in the 1980s and 1990s penned speeches for executive leaders at General Motors and Kraft Foods.[20] Perlman, who holds a PhD in linguistics, developed a method to capture the client's voice in a believable manner, based on a stylistic analysis of the client's profile. The analysis has three levels: 1) Verbal style, 2) Rhetorical techniques, and 3) Intellectual character.

The purpose of Perlman's stylistic profiling is to prepare a speech faithful to the personality of the speaker. The first level is an analysis of the client's language and style, in order to reproduce it: "Most stylisticians acknowledge that somehow you've got to replicate the speaker's syntax. However you can, make it sound like him or her. I'm talking in terms of really simple things like short sentences, long sentences, whatever."[21] As noted by Bruss, Perlman's focus on the speaker's individual style is distinctive from most ancient theories that develop the speaker's character, *ethopoeia*, in general. For instance, Aphthonius advises his students to develop characterization in a clear, concise, and fresh style, while Dionysius of Hallicarnassus recommends the use of clear and ordinary words.

The second level of Perlman's analysis, rhetorical techniques, relates to the client's way of making a point: "How does he or she like to prove things and explain things? Tell jokes? Give facts? Amazing facts? Historical references? Stories with anecdotes?"[22] Essentially, this part of the analysis is about argumentation. Once more, the originality of

---

20 Kristine S. Bruss, "Ghosting Authenticity: Characterization in Corporate Speechwriting," *Journal of Business and Technical Communication* 25, 2 (2011), 159-183. Bruss' information about Perlman is derived from interviews, in addition to Alan Perlman's book *Writing Great Speeches. Professional techniques you can use (*Boston, MA: Allyn & Bacon, 1998).

21 Bruss, "Ghosting Authenticity," 168.

22 Ibid.

Perlman's procedure – in comparison with the Classical theories of logography – lies in his effort to capture the individual personality of the speaker.

The third level concerns the speaker's intellectual character, an aspect that resembles *phronesis*, the speaker's practical wisdom – which is one of Aristotle's three categories of ethos. Yet Perlman's concept of intellectual character is rather specialized; it is attuned to the task of creating an authentic portrait through a display of knowledge. Perlman underlines that the portrayal of intellectual character depends on plausibility rather than on the client's actual knowledge. When deciding what would be appropriate for the speaker to speak about, it suffices that the speaker could plausibly have said it. According to Bruss, this rather liberal practice is in accordance with the practice of the ancient speechwriters:

> Dionysius described a similar approach taken by Lysias: "He often makes us believe in his client's good character by referring to the circumstances of his life and his parentage, and often again by describing his past actions and the principles governing them. And when the facts fail to provide him with such material, he creates his own moral tone, making his character seem by their speech to be trustworthy and honest."[23]

In sum, Perlman's method of analysis aims to capture the speaker's individuality by imitation. Compared to the two dominant topoi of speechwriting, it is obvious that Perlman's stylistic analysis – of verbal style, argumentative techniques, and intellectual character – is grounded in the topos which identifies style with subjectivity. Meanwhile, this is a rhetorical strategy which distinguishes itself from the strategies of the ancient practitioners, as I shall elaborate below.

23 Ibid., 174.

Ethopoeia: Dramatic Character

As noted by Bruss, Perlman's take on characterization resembles the ancient conceptof *ethopoeia*:

> which means character making, combining the Greek words *ethos* (character) and *poiein* (to make). In one of the first ancient accounts of *ethopoeia*, Dionysius of Halicarnassus praised the Athenian speechwriter Lysias: "I also ascribe to Lysias that most pleasing quality (*hê euprepestatê arête*, "most fitting virtue") which is generally called characterization (*êthopoeia*). I am quite unable to find a single person in this orator's speeches who is devoid of character or vitality. There are three departments or aspects in which this quality manifests itself: thought, language, and composition; and I declare him to be successful in all three."[24]

Although the categories identified by Dionysius – thought, language, and composition – are not identical to Perlman's, they overlap. Both methods suggest that the process of rhetorical characterization involves the interplay of several aspects.[25]

Bruss distinguishes *ethopoeia* from ethos, which is tied to persuasion and the creation of a favorable impression of the speaker through the display of wisdom, virtue, and goodwill. *Ethopoeia*, on the other hand, is a stylistic version of ethos, a creation of a character suitable to the speaking person. George A. Kennedy uses the term 'dramatic character' in his explanation of *ethopoeia*:

> Under Greek law it was customary for a man to plead his own case, though he might deliver a memorized oration which another had written and might introduce advocates who would

---

24 Ibid., 160-161.

25 Ibid., 161.

> speak for and after himself. In the former case ethos came to have a peculiar importance, for to achieve a successful effect the speech writer had to weave into the speech the actual character of the speaker, or at least he had to keep from saying things in a way that would be completely foreign to him. An old man and a young man must show quite different attitudes; a rich man would not think of things in the same way as a poor man. Such dramatic character is treated by Aristotle under style [...] and is called ethopoiia by critics.[26]

That the style (and attitude) of the speaker is categorized according to the social experience following from age and economic status corresponds with other theories of dramatic character in the rhetorical tradition. William Levring Devries summarizes the six categories which, according to Dionysius of Halicarnassos, are used to create *ethopoeia*: "This oratorical ethos involves six points, the race, family, age, principles, lot, and pursuits of the person."[27] As Kennedy's example shows, dramatic character depends on social typologies rather than individuality. For instance, Dionysius' last point concerns the speaker's profession; life turns out differently depending on whether you are a soldier or a doctor, and this experience shapes how and about what you will speak.

In comparison, Perlman's method aims to be 'faithful' to the speaker's own style, and it thus differs from both the approach of the Greek logographers and the theories of *ethopoeia*. Still, there are instances when modern and ancient speechwriters use the same strategy. Bruss recounts how Perlman began writing a speech for an executive by asking questions about the typologies of the profession as an inventional resource:

26 George Kennedy, *The Art of Persuasion in Greece* (Princeton, New Jersey: Princeton University Press, 1963), 91-92.

27 William Levering Devries, *Ethopoiia. A Rhetorical Study of the Types of Character in the Orations of Lysias* (Baltimore: John Murphy & Co., 1892), 10.

> Perlman's question, "What should the chairman say?" marks a typical starting point for dramatic characterization, drawing attention to the type of character for whom words are being chosen. In the ancient world, students began their ethopoetic exercises in the same way, prompted by questions such as, "What words would a man say to his wife when leaving on a journey? Or a general to his soldiers in time of danger?" (Theon, trans. 2003, 8.115). For *ethopoeia* to be effective, writers must understand what sort of words should be appropriate for different types of characters.[28]

In general, however, Perlman's stylistic analysis aims to reproduce the speaker's unique voice. His method differs, therefore, from the type-oriented style that centers on the speaker's role in a social context. This approach to speechwriting – that character is a construct relative to societal position and rank, demographic origin, economic status, and social relations – is on par with the style topos of speech as the dress of thought. Both have propriety as a point of orientation: The speech should be appropriate in relation to the social context and the speaker's social position rather than an authentic expression of the speaker's personality. [29]

---

28 Bruss, "Ghosting Authenticity," 164. George A. Kennedy, ed. and trans., *Progymnasmata. Greek Textbooks of Prose Composition and Rhetoric* (Atlanta, GA: Society of Biblical Literature, 2003). Conversely, more critics have stressed that individualized characterization occurs in ancient speeches, notably in those written by Lysias.

29 In Devries' paraphrase of Dionysius' treatise on Lysias, the paragraph about appropriateness is devoid of reflections on individuality: "To be appropriate to the speaker an oration must be adapted to his age, race, training, pursuits, mode of life and other characteristics. With respect to the audience the writer must consider whether the speech is addressed to the jury, the senate, the assembly, or the masses. Further, the style must vary with the parts of the speech as well as with its subject." Devries, *Ethopoiia*, 11. However, as Bruss has pointed out, this is a misinterpretation of Lysias, who makes such observations not in his discussion of

Constitutive Style

Obviously, the major critical issues of speechwriting fit hand in glove with Müller's stylistic topoi. Modern rhetorical criticism is predominantly founded on the topos of style as the man. And even though some critics attack the validity of this topos in relation to speechwriting, the critique is aimed at the ethical, qualitative, and social implications of speechwriting – and so is not an actual break with the idea that language and style could ideally express the personality of the speaker.

In addition, there are also significant examples of an understanding of speechwriting based on the topos of style as dress, sometimes even with the qualification that the speech should be tailor-made. This topos is far from incompatible with the type-oriented approach that can be found in most ancient theories on *ethopoeia*. If we follow this thought, an analysis of what it is possible for the speaker to speak about – and how – depends on a close analysis of the person's social position and experience, rather than on a special insight into the speaker's individual personality.

An objection to this theoretical development could be raised: When the dress metaphor is understood to be customized, it comes close to the other topos, of style as the man. A counter-argument would be that *ethopoeia*, the preparation of a speaker's character on the basis of an analysis of age, family, profession, etc., also resembles the process of customizing a garment. The crucial difference lies in the fact that the analysis of *ethopoeia* is based on social typologies, not a concern about an authentic representation of the speaker's individual style.

While the two topoi may be used to analyze and understand rhetorical theories about speechwriting, they cannot do so exhaustively. In the material I have discussed above, there are several examples of

---

ethopoeia, but of propriety. Kristine S. Bruss, "Persuasive *Ethopoeia* in Dionysius's *Lysias*," *Rhetorica: A Journal of the History of Rhetoric* 31, 1 (2013): 36.

theoretical and analytical 'residues,' mostly in the shape of inconsistencies, or contradictions. An example can be found in Bruss' divergent interpretations of Perlman's practice. At first, Perlman's focus on authenticity, on being 'true to nature,' is dominant. Bruss' conclusion is primarily founded on the topos of speech as the expression of the speaker's personality:

> The skillful ghost is a master of mimesis, attuned to character types, the distinctive characteristics of individual speakers, and conversational style. The result is the seemingly natural, artless expression of character, an aesthetic ideal valued by practitioners in ancient as well as contemporary time.[30]

Yet, at other times, Bruss articulates Perlman's practice as interpretative and based on a constitutive topos of style. This is evinced in the discussion concerning plausibility that I recounted above. In respect to creating the speaker's intellectual character, Perlman is on par with his ancient predecessors in a fairly liberal interpretation of what the speaker might plausibly know, rather than what he positively knows.

That speechwriting is a constitutive practice is not, however, completely foreign to Bruss. She suggests as much when she cautiously joins the ethical discussion that has preoccupied other rhetorical critics: "But when does effective characterization cross an ethical line? As this analysis shows, authenticity, or true-to-life portrayal, is a rhetorical creation."[31] The last sentence indicates that authenticity is a rhetorical construction – a radical thought that is out of tune with the general understanding of the speech as an expression of the speaker's personality. Onsberg and Jamieson's interpretations of the Kennedy-Sorensen collaboration also point in this direction. Rather than viewing style as a fitting item of clothing or a sign of Kennedy's identity, both rhe-

---

30 Bruss, "Ghosting Authenticity," 177.

31 Ibid., 178.

torical critics conclude that Kennedy's public speaking was actually a creation of character.

On this basis I am able to conclude that the rhetorical criticism on speechwriting is in need of a third topos, in addition to the two developed by Müller in *Topik des Stilbegriffs*. This third topos for speechwriting for others is founded on a theory of constitutive rhetoric which perceives language as the creator of meaning and identity. That speechwriting is constitutive does not, however, turn the logographer into a writer of fiction who is free to invent the speaker's attitudes, language, and character. Far from it; the speechwriter must create the speaker's character on the basis of existing narratives that either are or possess the potential to be shared by the speaker and the audience. Still, this topos gives the speechwriter the rhetorical agency to rearticulate existing subject-positions rather than simply reproducing them. Furthermore, the constitutive topos enables the critic to inspect logograpy in another light: Speechwriting is not a simple reproduction of an already established stereotype; it is a performative and dynamic process allowing for new choices, new roads, and new actions.

Speechwriting as Cooking

As I described in chapter one, Müller discusses how the most common reception of 'style is the man' is an anachronism, a misinterpretation of Buffon's conceptual context. Nevertheless, Müller acknowledges the significance of the wording because it works; it easily identifies the idea that style is an incarnation of a thought or person. As Müller explains, his own use of the concept of topos is founded on the traditional double nature of topoi, which refers to both the central argument and thought and to a well-known common expression.[32] It follows that the significance and expediency of a topos depends on the pregnancy of its formulation.

---

32 Müller, *Topik des Stilbegriffs*, 4.

Inspired by this thought, my proposition of a new topos must offer some kind of forceful wording, such as an apt analogy. The literature on speechwriting is already plentiful in analogies, and Bormann contributes with a few of his own. He compares speechwriting with a TV quiz show that has been fixed: "the two situations are analogous. In the one instance the public was told that bank vaults protected the integrity of the questions; in the other, the speaker pretends to be delivering his own ideas in his own language."[33] Like the TV quiz show, speechwriting is a fixed match, and success or failure is totally dependent on the audience's gullibility. Therefore, to Bormann, the apologists' excuse that everyone knew that the quiz show was fixed is no good. The same argument applies to speechwriting: "Everyone does not know that speeches are ghostwritten."[34]

Conversely, in defense of professional speechwriting it has been argued that the practice is no more ethically harmful than competent stenography. Comparisons with the shining of shoes, the booking of hotel rooms, or the carrying of luggage enforce the argument that speechwriting is an essentially trivial business. Other analogies mentioned by Bormann compare speechwriting to different academic genres or situations – scientific articles, student assignments, or supervising a Master's thesis. These comparisons are used to discuss the fine line between a writer's own product and the usurpation of that of others.

The introduction of a constitutive topos, however, calls for something other, if not entirely new. To this purpose, I propose the analogy of *speechwriting as cooking*. This topos, which is also mentioned in passing by Bormann, is borrowed from Plato's dialogue *Gorgias*, in which Socrates attacks rhetoric for not being a craft. Instead, rhetoric is merely a practice, a knack for producing pleasure and gratification; in short, it is flattery.[35]

---

33 Bormann, "Ethics of Ghostwritten Speeches," 262.

34 Ibid.

35 Plato, *Gorgias*, transl. Terence Irwin, Clarendon Plato Series (Oxford: Clarendon Press, 1979), 462e–463c, 31.

Without subscribing to Plato's condemnation of rhetoric, I believe cooking to be a useful metaphor to provide speechwriting with the qualities of a creative and constitutive practice. Like the cook, the speechwriter has ingredients that she prepares to the best of her ability, and from this process something new emerges. Some of it depends on the quality of ingredients, some on the capability of the cook and the kitchen staff, and some on the cook's willingness to meet the expectations of the diners – and quite a lot on her talent to surpass them! Last but not least, a successful meal demands a sense of timing. Other less concrete qualities include taste, aesthetics, and the endeavor to provide an unforgettable culinary experience that no one would dare to miss. Indeed, cooking seems to be the perfect metaphor for speechwriting.

Instead of probing the theoretical developments in a case study, I shall exemplify the practical effects in a discussion that aims if not to formulate concrete prescriptions for speechwriting, then at least to bolster logographers in the creative phase. To me, speechwriting as cooking is the preferred topos, because it allows for something new to happen in the process of writing and speaking. It is not tied to certain social typologies; nor is it obliged to replicate the dramatic character of earlier speeches – for all we know, the persona portrayed in earlier speeches might be closer to (the taste or prejudices of) former speechwriters and advisors than to the speaker's personality.

Speechwriting as cooking is a constitutive topos which enables the speechwriter to shape individual character in the creative process. For the speech to succeed, it must produce a plausible character which coheres with or counters existing narratives about the speaker. In order to do so, the speech must combine known components – while it may be desirable to leave others out. It will have to dramatize the character in ways that do not conspicuously contradict the speaker's public image, the speaker's way of acting in informal settings, or public interpretations by friends and foes. Yet it is crucial to the constitutive outlook that absolute loyalty to existing narratives is no requirement. The cook does not have to repeat last night's menu in every detail.

Rather, it is possible to reshape character and to create new sentiments, new policies, and new public opinions.

Another result of approaching speechwriting from a constitutive topos is that it makes the concern about ethics less exigent. As Bormann was aware, the ethical implications of ghostwriting were thoroughly enmeshed in an interest in the speaker's biography, or in stylistic terms: in the Romantic topos of style as the perfect expression of the speaker's inner state. However, when viewing speechwriting as a constitutive practice, the interest in the speaker's biography is replaced by an effort to create a strong and persuasive rhetor persona. In this respect, the constitutive topos coheres with the ideal embedded in the concept of *ethopoeia* and the topos of style as dress; in both *aptum* is the primary focus. However, that ethics does not control the constitutive topos of speechwriting does not preclude it altogether either.

Most importantly perhaps, the constitutive topos enables the rhetorical critic to raise her eyes from the dynamics of the ratio of speech and speaker and think about other, more functional, aspects of style in speechwriting – notably, the rhetorical effects of using style to argumentative and strategic ends. The consideration of style in this respect enables the critic to reflect on other norms and ideals of speechwriting.[36]

---

36 In the literature on speechwriting, in fact, two almost opposite ideals have guided speechwriters for American presidents in the second half of the twentieth century: Kennedy's eloquent and Reagan's conversational style. For further reading, see Jette Barnholdt Hansen, Amos Kiewe, Jens E. Kjeldsen, & Marie Lund, *Speechwriting* (forthcoming).

CONCLUSION

While the first part of this book was devoted to definition, conceptual development, and theoretical overview, Part Two consists of three separate investigations of particular styles. Chapters four and five contain close readings that strive towards an interpretational dynamic where insights produced by analyzing the artifact from a specific conceptual focus reflect back on the concept, which is in turn developed, and perhaps even reinterpreted. Thus, the readings have both rhetorical discourse and rhetorical theory as their objects. In this respect, the approach to speechwriting in chapter six differs; it is not a close textual analysis of a specific, critically selected corpus of rhetorical discourse and context. Instead, it is a theoretical development of a particular rhetorical critical topic. Its investigation of speechwriting revolves around the three topoi of style as it discusses and criticizes existing theories of speechwriting. In this way, it exemplifies my earlier argument for the value of maintaining three topoi of style in the critical practice.

Meanwhile, the three stylistic topoi are not the center of the critical investigations in the two preceding chapters. The readings of particular stylistic repertoires in chapters four and five are by and large carried by the notion of constitutive style. Both feminine style and provocative style are concepts congenial with postmodern rhetorical theories, and both correspond with the third topos of style. This does not mean, however, that the topoi of style as man and style as dress are not implied. In chapter four, the rhetoric of politicians who both speak in a feminine style and argue for an essentialist perception of gender may well be associated with the topos of style as man. The topos of style as dress, on the other hand, may be detected in the chair's ironic attitude to storytelling as a feature of feminine style. Similarly in chapter five, the main conceptual development of provocative style is founded on a topos of constitutive and strategic style. However, the other stylistic topoi may easily be identified. In his stylistic imitation of biblical prophesies, Gaarder assumes that a mockery of style will be perceived as a seminal religious and cultural offence. Apparently, the assumption of stylistic identification is correct: The stylistic parody is indeed an effective provocation. The other topos, style as dress, appears in Gaarder's half-hearted apology when he tries to separate style and passion from the substantive argument.

I shall not give a full summary of the first three chapters here, but I will recapture some of the main points of Part One and tie them to the readings and critical discussions in Part Two. But first, I shall give a summary of the investigations in chapters four, five, and six. The common thread in the Conclusion will be critical reflections, in respect to both insights and points of criticism.

To sum up my critical inquiry into the feminine style, it analyzes how a fairly consistent body of argumentative and stylistic features is sought to constitute an audience of politically empowered women. The analysis questions the effect and expedience of such a rhetorical strategy. The contextual transfer from one historical and cultural setting to another seems to have worn down much of the power of feminine style. Perhaps the analysis even confirms the deficiencies that some critics claim are immanent features. If so, the feminine style is, in fact, not as empowering as earlier critics had envisioned it to be, but rather a fairly conservative strategy either preservative of the status quo or limiting of rhetorical and political options. If this is a valid interpretation, the evaluation of the Aarhus debate turns out to be the perfect reversal of Campbell's assessment of Hillary Clinton's failed rhetorical strategy: In the Danish case, the lack of resonance in the audience testifies to a fairly progressive society.

The critical merit of the investigation is that it sheds light on the debaters' strategic purposes as well as their ideological motives.

Moreover, the study enables us to draw some conclusions about the effect – or at least on a critical basis and with an analytical backing to explain why this particular rhetorical choice does not seem to be a very convincing persuasive strategy. However, the close reading provides us with knowledge about more than the rhetorical artefacts. The insights produced by the study reflect back on the concept of feminine style and thereby add to our understanding of its realm and limitations.

Like the feminine style, the provocative style is epistemologically related to postmodern rhetorical theories and founded on a topos of constitutive style. Although the idea of a provocative style is hardly innovative, the conceptualization of provocation as a particular rhetorical-stylistic strategy is mine. The critical aim of the conceptualization is to analyze and describe the way provocative devices work – and through a careful and comprehensive account of text and context to be able to evaluate it. My investigation unfolds on three levels: as a reading of a particular case, as a conceptual development, and as a meta-critical discussion of moral evaluation in rhetorical criticism. With this critical approach, I distance myself from a tradition of normative judgment predominant in argumentation studies – as well as in Danish normative rhetoric – where universal norms are made the parameter for assessing the practice of public dialogue. Instead, I make the analytical and critical findings of the debate both the object and basis of critical judgment. Thus, rhetorical analysis of the provocative devices and the formation of the actual debate – how the participants form and perform their position, and how the exchange develops – is the ground on which I make an appreciatory evaluation of the debate. On a general level, I insist that rhetorical critical evaluations are based on close textual analysis of rhetorical practice rather than on positive or negative assumptions about effects.

In chapter six, I fine-comb rhetorical theories of speechwriting, especially in relation to *ethopoeia*, the composition of the speaker's voice and character. Close readings of some of the essential theoretical texts on speechwriting confirm that my three-facetted cut of style is nothing less than an organizing principle. Although I acknowledge the widespread use of the topoi of style as man and style as dress, I strike a blow for the third, constitutive topos as the more beneficial. I do this primarily to enable theorists and practitioners alike to view and articulate speechwriting as a creative process. If speechwriting were viewed less like a set assignment, if speechwriters were granted more authority over the writing process and the written product, higher quality public speeches would be the likely outcome.

To briefly return to Part One, it may be characterized as an investigation of style as sign, or rather, of three independent interpretations of the sign *style*. Wolfgang G. Müller is responsible for the first two, while the last is my own invention. The first understands style as external to substance – whether the substance is considered to be of an argumentative or ideational nature. The associated dress-metaphor supplies it with a social dimension, a demand for social skills, or more specifically, a competence to read a particular social situation and 'dress,' behave, and speak, to the occasion. The second interpretation views style as the formal embodiment of the speaker or writer's personality. Style is a display of some essence – of a subject's individuality, a philosophical idea, or the spirit of a shared, cultural identity – which it represents genuinely and loyally.

According to the third interpretation, which I prefer, style is textual in the sense that it is exists in text without being anchored beyond text. Instead, it is thought to be constitutive of so-called substantial qualities such as meaning, ideas, argumentation, political action, cultural values, identity, and gender. These qualities are inscribed textually or created in performative acts and gestures. Thus, constitutive style has a productive and inventive potential that may be employed strategically, but also testifies to the way individuals are shaped by their social and cultural milieu.

As noted in the Sub-conclusion, it is often analytically productive to use all three stylistic topoi and test their interpretative perspectives. When the different topoi fall into place, interpretative lines enable the critic to understand the functions of style. I share this critical move with Müller, who documented an occasional historical co-existence of the topoi of style as man and style as dress, yet considered them incompatible. In addition to Müller's theory I introduced the topos of constitutive style, and – contrary to Müller's – my critical investigation has established that all three topoi are actively practised in discourse. Even so, I do not consider the three topoi equally important, but favor the third, constitutive understanding of style.

As argued earlier, I believe it is crucial to maintain a conceptual stringency if theoretical findings are to have an effect on critical and communicative practice. In order critically to detect the function of stylistic strategies or to release their creative power, the defining lines of the topoi must be kept straight. If the lines are blurred, the theoretical perspectives will soon fade, as will their communicative and didactic potential.

Some points of critique may be raised against my theory of style and its methodological employment. In a study of the process of political speechwriting for others, Mette Stoltenberg has argued that all three topoi are valid and useful. Indeed, a preference for one topos at the expense of others is a theoretical move that runs counter to the rhetorical practice of political speechwriting.[1] I acknowledge that the conceptual developments of the project merit a degree of use in critical and creative practices. Theoretical stringency may look less brilliant after an encounter with the untidy practice of real life rhetoric. Even so, I must maintain that the stylistic topoi are more than rhetorical devices that the critic may choose to combine if they fit the case under study. Rather, I consider the three topoi to be fundamentally different epistemological outlooks that any criticism of rhetorical style will have to position itself in relation to.

I take this discussion to be illustrative of an argument I made earlier. In the introduction I described my investigation as a re-theorizing of rhetoric, and proposed to strengthen the theoretical reflection on

---

1 Mette Stoltenberg Hansen, "Hvem har ordet? En retorisk analyse af taleskrivning for en anden i danske ministerier og kommuner" (unpublished Master's thesis, Aarhus University, 2014).

rhetoric in order for it to become the solid basis for a critique of practice. Although I understand rhetorical criticism as a meeting between theoretical concepts and discursive practice where both are explored and developed, I believe that the theoretical reflections should set the defining framework for the interaction. In fact, this idea has been the gist of my study of rhetorical style.

Another objection to my theory of the three topoi of style could be that it is an instance of analytical 'category-fit' – not unlike the theories built around two or four rhetorical figures that I criticized in chapter two. Indisputably, such critique is appropriate, and my only defense is a modification: I do not aspire to make it a 'general rhetoric,' but simply to limit my analytic enterprise to rhetorical style. My aim has been to structure and illuminate, and I have argued and demonstrated just how flexible and dynamic the analytical categories of styles may be.

In my least humble moments, I see my contribution as a diamond cutting. I revive an old metaphor for style, of course, but in my reinterpretation, the diamond is taken to be more than a piece of jewelry. It is a raw material which is worked up to cut sharper and shine brighter, and in the making, its own creative and manufacturing properties are perfected. While a diamond is appreciated for its beauty and preciousness of clarity and color, it is also valued for its solid weight – its carat. Style is a precious stone, a hard rock hopefully made stronger in its critical processing.

WORKS CITED

Aarhus Kommune. https://www.aarhus.dk/da/politik/Byraadet/En-plads-i-Aarhus-Byraad/Kvinder-i-byraadet.aspx. Accessed February 6, 2017.

Amossy, Ruth. "The Function of Polemical Discourse in the Public Sphere." In *The Responsibilities of Rhetoric*, edited by Michelle Smith and Barbara Warnick. Long Grove: Waveland Press, 2010: 52-61.

Andersen, Øivind. *I retorikkens hage*. Oslo: Universitetsforlaget, 1995.

Aristotle. *On Rhetoric. A Theory of Civic Discourse*, translated by G. A. Kennedy. Oxford: Oxford University Press, 2007.

Aristotle. *Poetics* in *The Basic Works of Aristotle*, edited by Richard McKeon. New York: The Modern Library, 2001.

Barck, Karlheinz et al., eds. *Ästhetische Grundbegriffe*, vols 1-5. Stuttgart: Metzler, 2000-2005.

Barthes, Roland. "L'ancienne rhétorique. Aide-mémoire." *Communications* 16, *Recherche rhétoriques* (1994): 254-333.

Biesecker, Barbara. "Rethinking the Rhetorical Situation from within the Thematic of Différance." In *Contemporary Rhetorical Theory*, edited by John Louis Lucaites et al. New York: The Guildford Press, 1999: 232-249.

Black, Edwin. "The Second Persona." In *Contemporary Rhetorical Theory*, edited by John Louis Lucaites et al. New York: The Guildford Press, 1999: 331-340.

Black, Max. *Models and Metaphors. Studies in Language and Philosophy.* Ithaca: Cornell University Press, 1972.

Black, Max. "More about Metaphor." In *Metaphor and Thought*, edited by Andrew Ortony. Cambridge: Cambridge University Press, 1993: 19-41.

Blankenship, Jane and Deborah C. Robson. "A 'Feminine Style' in Women's Political Discourse: An Exploratory Essay." *Communication Quarterly* 43, 3 (1995): 353-366.

Bono. "More leaders slipping up than stepping up for Africa at this year's G8." Press Release, August 6, 2007. www.data.org/node/148/print.

Bono. "Speech at the Labour Party Conference." September 9, 2004, http://www.atu2.com/news/transcript-of-bonos-speech-at-labour-party-conference.html. Accessed February 6, 2017.

Borchorst, Anette. "27 procent kvinder i dansk lokalpolitik – hvad er problemet?" In *Kvinder i kommunalpolitik 1909-2009. Festskrift for 100 år med kvinders valgret*, edited by Jytte Larsen, 2009, http://kvinfo.dk/2015/kvinder-i-kommunalpolitik-1909-2009-festskrift-100-aar-med-kvinders-valgret. Accessed February 6, 2017.

Bormann, Ernest G. "Ghostwriting and the Rhetorical Critic." *Quarterly Journal of Speech*, 46, 3 (1960): 284-288.

Bormann, Ernest G. "Ethics of Ghostwritten Speeches." *Quarterly Journal of Speech*, 47, 3 (1961): 262-267.

Bradlee, Benjamin C. *Conversations with Kennedy*. New York: W.W. Norton, 1975.

Brummett, Barry. *A Rhetoric of Style*. Carbondale: Southern Illinois University Press, 2008.

Bruss, Kristine S. "Ghosting Authenticity: Characterization in Corporate Speechwriting," *Journal of Business and Technical Communication* 25, 2 (2011): 159-183.

Bruss, Kristine S. "Persuasive *Ethopoeia* in Dionysius's *Lysias*," *Rhetorica: A Journal of the History of Rhetoric* 31, 1 (2013): 34-57.

Burke, Kenneth. *A Rhetoric of Motives*. Berkeley: University of California Press, 1965.

Butler, Judith P. *Gender Trouble*. New York: Routledge, 1990.

Butler, Judith. *The Psychic Life of Power. Theories in Subjection*. Palo Alto: Stanford University Press, 1997.

Campbell, Karlyn Kohrs. *Man Cannot Speak for Her.* Contributions in Women's Studies, vol. 1. New York: Greenwood Press, 1989.

Cambell, Karlyn Kohrs. "The Discursive Performance of Femininity." *Rhetoric & Public Affairs* 1, 1 (1998): 4-19.

Campbell, Karlyn Kohrs. "The Rhetoric of Women's Liberation: An Oxymoron". *Contemporary Rhetorical Theory: A Reader*, edited by John Louis Lucaites et al. New York: The Guilford Press (1999): 397-410.

Campbell, Karlyn Kohrs and Kathleen Hall Jamieson. *Presidents Creating the Presidency. Deeds Done in Words*. Chicago: University of Chicago Press, 2008.

Charland, Maurice. "Constitutive Rhetoric: The Case of the *Peuple Québécois.*" *The Quarterley Journal of Speech* 73, 2 (1987): 133-150.

Charland, Maurice. "Constitutive rhetoric." In *Encylopedia of rhetoric*, edited by Thomas O. Sloane. Oxford: Oxford University Press, 2001: 616-619.

Conley, Thomas. *Toward a Rhetoric of Insult*. Chicago: The University of Chicago Press, 2010.

Cowley, Abraham. *The Complete Works in Verse and Prose II*, edited by Alexander B. Grosart. Hildesheim, 1969.

Crick, Nathan. "The Sophistical Attitude and the Invention of Rhetoric." *Quarterly Journal of Speech* 96, 1 (2010): 25-45.

Demosthenes. *Speeches 18 and 19*, translated by Harvey Yunis. Austin: University of Texas Press, 2005.

Devries, William Levering. Ethopoiia. *A Rhetorical Study of the Types of Character in the Orations of Lysias*. Baltimore: John Murphy & Co., 1892.

Dow, Bonnie J. and Mari Boor Tonn. "'Feminine Style' and Political Judgment in the Rhetoric of Ann Richards." *Quarterly Journal of Speech* 79, 3 (1993): 286-302.

Dryden, John. *Of Dramatic Poesy and Other Critical Essays II*, edited by George Watson. London: Everyman's Library, 1971.

Eide, Tormod. *Retorisk leksikon*. Oslo: Spartacus forlag, 1999.

Einhorn, Lois J. "The Ghosts Unmasked: A Review of Literature on Speechwriting," *Communication Quarterly* 30, 1 (1982): 41-47.

Fahnestock, Jeanne. *Rhetorical Figures in Science*. Oxford: Oxford University Press, 2002.

Fahnestock, Jeanne. *Rhetorical Style. The Uses of Language in Persuasion*. Oxford: Oxford University Press 2011.

Fairlie, Henry Fairlie. *The Kennedy Promise*. New York: Dell Publishing, 1972.

"Famous Scotts: Sir Walter Scott (1771-1832)." July 1, 2006. http://www.rampantscotland.com/famous/blfamscott.htm. Accessed February 6, 2017.

Ferguson, Robert. *The Interest of Reason in Religion, with the Import & Use of Scripture-Metaphors; and The Nature of the Union Betwixt Christ & Believers*. London, 1675.

Fix, Ulla, Andreas Gardt and Joachim Knape, eds. *Rhetorik und Stilistik: ein internationals Handbuch historicher und systematischer Forschung/ Rhetoric and Stylistics: an international handbook of historical and systematic research*, vols 1-2. Berlin: Gruyter, 2008-2009.

Færch, Christina Holst. "En særdeles parfumeret retorik. Smædeversets retorik og politisk dyd i 1700-tallets Danmark." *Rhetorica Scandinavica* 57 (2011): 60-78.

Gaarder, Jostein. "God's Chosen People." The Simon Wiesenthal Center Homepage. http://www.wiesenthal.com/site/apps/nlnet/content2.aspx?c=lsKWLbPJLnF&b=4442247&ct=5850849. Accessed February 6, 2017.

Gaarder, Jostein. "Forsøk på Klargjøring." *Aftenposten*. August 12, 2006. http://www.aftenposten.no/meninger/kronikk/Forsok-pa-klargjoring-393867b.html. Accessed February 6, 2017.

Genette, Gérard. "La rhétorique restreinte." *Communications* 16, *Recherches rhétoriques* (1994): 233-253.

Gray, Bennison. *Style – The Problem and Its Solution*. The Hague: Mouton, 1969.

Gumbrecht, Hans Ulrich. "Schwindende Stabilität der Wirklichkeit. Eine Geschichte des Stilbegriffs." In *Stil. Geschichten und Funktionen eines kulturwissenschaftlichen Diskurselements*, edited by H. U. Gumbrecht and K. L. Pfeiffer. Frankfurt am Main: Suhrkamp Taschenbuch Verlag, 1986.

Gumbrecht, Hans Ulrich and K. Ludwig Pfeiffer, eds. *Stil. Geschichten und Funktionen eines kulturwissenschaftlichen Diskurselements*. Frankfurt am Main: Suhrkamp Taschenbuch Verlag, 1986.

Hansen, Mette Stoltenberg. "Hvem har ordet? En retorisk analyse af taleskrivning for en anden i danske ministerier og kommuner" (unpublished Master's thesis, Aarhus University, 2014).

Hansen, Jette Barnholdt, Amos Kiewe, Jens E. Kjeldsen, and Marie Lund. *Speechwriting* (forthcoming).

Hariman, Robert. *Political Style. The Artistry of Power*. Chicago: The University of Chicago Press, 1995.

Hauser, Gerard A. *Vernacular Voices: The Rhetoric of Publics and Public Spheres*. Columbia: University of South Carolina Press, 1999.

Hauser, Gerard A. *Introduction to Rhetorical Theory* (2nd edition). Prospect Heights: Waveland Press, 2002.

Hebdige, Dick. *Subculture. The Meaning of Style*. Taylor & Francis e-Library, [1979] 2002.

Hochmuth, Marie. "The Criticism of Rhetoric." In *A History and Criticism of American Public Address*, vol. 3, edited by Marie Hochmuth. New York: McGraw-Hill, 1955.

Hochmuth Nichols, Marie. *Rhetoric and Criticism*. Baton Rouge: Louisiana State University Press, 1972.

Holst, Hanne-Vibeke. "Du er fucking sexistisk, Niarn!", *Politiken*. November 13, 2004.

Jakobson, Roman. "Two Aspects of Language and Two Types of Aphasic Disturbances." In *Selected Writings II*. The Hague: Mouton, 1971.

Jamieson, Kathleen Hall. *Eloquence in an Electronic Age. The Transformation of Political Speechmaking*. Oxford: Oxford University Press, 1988.

Jarratt, Susan. *Rereading the Sophists. Classical Rhetoric Refigured*. Carbondale: Southern Illinois University Press, 1991.

Jasinski, James. *Sourcebook on Rhetoric. Key Concepts in Contemporary Rhetorical Studies*. Thousand Oaks: Sage Publications, 2001.

Jokeren. *Gigolo Jesus*. Flamingo Records, 2005.

Johnson, Danette Ifert. "Feminine Style in Presidential Debate Discourse, 1960-2000." *Communication Quarterly* 53, 1 (2005): 3-20.

Jong, Jaap de and Bas Andesweg. "All's Well that Ends Well: The Problem of Peroratio in Ministerial Speeches." In *Rhetorical Aspects of Discourse in Present-Day Society*, edited by Lotte Dam, Lise-Lotte Holmgreen and Jeanne Strunck. Newcastle: Cambridge Scholars Publishing, 2008: 31-49.

Jong, Jaap de and Bas Andesweg. "Professionalizing Speech Production. Changes in 15 Years of Ministerial Speeches." In *Bending Opinion: Essays on Persuasion in the Public Domain*, edited by Ton van Haaften et al. Leiden: Leiden University Press, 2012: 159-183.

Jørgensen, Charlotte. "Debattens væsen og uvæsen. Om fjendtlighed i den offentlige debat." *Retorik Studier* 10 (1995): 3-43.

Kennedy, George. *The Art of Persuasion in Greece*. Princeton, New Jersey: Princeton University Press, 1963.

Kennedy, George A. *Quintilian*. New York: Twayne Publishers, 1969.

Kennedy, George A., ed. and trans. *Progymnasmata. Greek Textbooks of Prose Composition and Rhetoric*. Atlanta, GA: Society of Biblical Literature, 2003.

Kjær, Ulrik. "Kvinder i kommunalpolitik – er grænset nået?" *Kvinder, køn og forskning* 10, 1 (2001): 68-78.

Klujeff, Marie Lund. "Folketingets åbningstaler, 1953-" http://danmarkshistorien.dk/leksikon-og-kilder/vis/materiale/folketingets-aabningstaler-1953/?no_cache=1&cHash=88118ae48ecfc8d91ffdaa00f60e9bee. Accessed February 6, 2017.

Klujeff, Marie Lund. "Retoriske figurer og stil som argumentation." *Rhetorica Scandinavica* 45, (2008): 28-48.

Klujeff, Marie Lund. "Rhetorical Figures and Style as Argumentation." In *Scandinavian Studies in Rhetoric. Rhetorica Scandinavica 1997-2010*, edited by Jens E. Kjeldsen and Jan Grue. Ödåkra: Retorikförlaget, 2011: 308-329.

Klujeff, Marie Lund. "Provocative Style: The Gaarder Debate Example." In *Rhetorical Citizenship and Public Deliberation*, edited by Christian Kock and Lisa S. Villadsen. University Park: The Pennsylvania State University Press, 2012: 101-114.

Knape, Joachim. "Elocutio (griech. λέξιξ, léxis, φφάσιδ, phrásis; dt. rednerischer Ausdruck, Stil; engl. diction, locution, elocution; frz. Elocution; ital. elocuzione)." In *Historisches Wörterbuch der Rhetorik*, vol. 2, edited by Gert Ueding. Darmstadt: Wissenschaftliche Buchgesellschaft, 1994: 1022-1083.

Knudsen, Tim. "Statsministeren har ordet." *Information*. October 5, 2009.

Koesten, Joy, and Robert C. Rowland. "The Rhetoric of Atonement." *Western Journal of Communication* 55 (2004): 68-87.

Krag, Jens Otto. Opening Address. October 3, 1972. http://danmarkshistorien.dk/leksikon-og-kilder/vis/materiale/jens-otto-krags-s-tale-ved-folketingets-aabning-1972/?no_cache=1&cHash=c90ba371e59c1de84015c20fcd07050a. Accessed January 31, 2017.

Kristol, William. "Anti-Judaism." *Weekly Standard*, September 11, 2006.

Krogløkke, Charlotte and Karen Foss. "'Sørg hellere for en solid tremmeseng.'" *Rhetorica Scandinavica* 42 (2007): 4-19.

Lakoff, George and Mark Johnson. *Metaphors We Live By*. Chicago: The University of Chicago Press, 1980.

Lakoff, George and Mark Turner. *More than Cool Reason. A Field Guide to Poetic Metaphor*. Chicago: University of Chicago Press, 1989.

Lakoff, George. "The Contemporary Theory of Metaphor." In *Metaphor and Thought*, edited by Andrew Ortony. Cambridge: Cambridge University Press, 1993: 202-251.

Lemche, Gyrithe: Speech at Dansk Kvindesamfund's meeting on the right to vote, Rosenborg Have, June 28, 1908. http://danmarkshistorien.dk/leksikon-og-kilder/vis/materiale/gyrithe-lemches-tale-ved-valgretsmoede-i-rosenborg-have-28-juni-1908/?no_cache=1. Accessed February 6, 2017.

Lund, Marie. "Taleskrivning og stil." *Rhetorica Scandinavica* 65 (2013): 25-39.

Lund, Marie. "Retorisk stil." In *Retorikkens aktualitet. Grundbog i retorisk kritik*, edited by Marie Lund and Hanne Roer. København: Hans Reitzels forlag, 2014: 165-190.

Lund, Marie and Hanne Roer, eds. *Retorikkens aktualitet. Grundbog i retorisk kritik*, København: Hans Reitzels forlag, 2014.

Lykkeberg, Rune. "Et spørgsmål om stil." *Information*. March 27-28, 2010.

Lykkeberg, Rune. "Statsministerens stil." *Information*. January 6, 2012.

Mackin, James A., Jr. "Schismogenesis and Community: Pericles' Funeral Oration." *Quarterly Journal of Speech* 77, 3 (1991): 251-262.

Maffesoli, Michel. *The Contemplation of the World: Figures of Community Style*. Minneapolis: University of Minnesota Press, 1996.

Mattsson, Annie Mattsson. "Den tyranniske teaterkungen. Smædelser mot Gustaf III," *Rhetorica Scandinavica* 57 (2011): 93-112.

Mayer, H. "Stillehre, Stilistik (lat. bene dicendi praecepta, elocutionis ratio; eng. Stylistics; frz. Stylistique; its. Stilica)." In *Historisches Wörterbuch der Rhetorik*, vol. 9, edited by Gert Ueding. Darmstadt: Wissenschaftliche Buchgesellschaft, 2007: 1-83.

Medhurst, Martin J. "Ghostwritten Speeches: Ethics isn't the only Lesson," *Communication Education* 36 (1987): 241-249.

Medhurst, Martin J. "Introduction. Presidential Speechwriting: Ten Myths That Plague Modern Scholarship." In *Presidential Speechwriting. From the New Deal to the Reagan Revolution and Beyond*, edited by Kurt Ritter og Martin J. Medhurst. College Station: Texas A & M University Press, 2003: 3-19.

Merleau-Ponty, Maurice. *Signes*. Paris: Gallimard, 1960.

Murphy, James J. "*Topos* and *Figura*: Historical cause and effect?" In *De Ortu Grammaticae. Studies in Medieval Grammar and Linguistic Theory in Memory of Jan Pinborg*, edited by G. L. Bursill-Hall et al. Amsterdam: John Benjamins Publishing Company, 1990.

Müller, Wolfgang G. *Topik des Stilbegriffs. Zur Geschicte des Stilverständnisses von der Antike bis zur Gegenwart*. Darmstadt: Wissenschaftliche Buchgesellschaft, 1981.

Müller, Wolfgang G. "Style." In *Encyclopedia of Rhetoric*, edited by Thomas O. Sloane. Oxford: Oxford University Press, 2001: 745-757.

Müller, Wolfgang G. "Epochenstil/Zeitstil." In *Rhetorik und Stilistik: Ein internationals Handbuch historischer und systematischer Forschung / Rhetoric and Stylistics: An International Handbook of Historical and Systematic Research*, vols. 1-2, edited by Ulla Fix, Andreas Gardt, and Joachim Knape. Berlin: Gruyter, 2008-2009: 1271-1285.

Neumann, U. "Invektive (griech. Ψόγος, psógos; διαβολή, diabolé; lat. vituperatio, oratio, invectivs; engl., frz. invective; ital. invettiva)." In *Historisches Wörterbuch der Rhetorik*, vol. 4, edited by Gert Ueding. Darmstadt: Wissenschaftliche Buchgesellschaft, 1998: 549-561.

Niarn. "Jeg er fucking realistisk, Hanne!", *Politiken*. November 20 2004.

Nielsen, Peter Heyn. "Statsministeren fik ordet – historien om den danske åbningstale." *Økonomi og politik* 85 (2012): 87-99.

Olbrechts-Tyteca, Lucie. *Le comique de discours*. Bruxelles: Inst. De Sociologie, 1974.

Ong, Walter. *Ramus. Method and the Decay of Dialogue*. Cambridge, Mass: Octagon Books, 1958.

Onsberg, Merete. "En mand er en mand, og et ord er et ord – men hvis ord er mandens? Om nogle retoriske problemer ved den politiske taleskrivning." *Retorikstudier* 11 (1998): 24-61.

Ortony, Andrew, ed. *Metaphor and Thought*. Cambridge: Cambridge University Press, 1993.

Parry-Giles, Shawn J. and Trevor Parry-Giles. "Gendered Politics and Presidential Image Construction: A Reassessment of the 'Feminine Style.'" *Communication Monographs* 63 (1996): 337-353.

Perelman, Chaim and Lucie Olbrechts-Tyteca. *The New Rhetoric. A Treatise on Argumentation*. Notre Dame: University of Notre Dame Press, 1969.

Perelman, Chaïm. *The New Rhetoric and the Humanities*. Dordrecht: D. Reidel Publishing Company, 1979.

Perlman, Alan. *Writing Great Speeches. Professional techniques you can use*. Boston, MA: Allyn & Bacon, 1998.

Pitkin, Hanna: *The Concept of Representation*. Berkeley: University of California Press, 1967

Plato. *Gorgias*, translated by Terence Irwin. Clarendon Plato Series. Oxford: Clarendon Press, 1979.

Pritsch, Sylvia. *Rhetorik des Subjekts. Zur textuellen Konstruktion des Subjekts in feministischen und anderen postmoderne Diskursen*. Bielefeld: transcript verlag, 2008.

Quintilian. *The Instituio Oratoria of Quintilian I–IV.* The Loeb Classical Library, 1953.

Rand, Erin. "An Inflammatory Fag and a Queer Form: Larry Kramer, Polemics, and Rhetorical Agency." *Quarterly Journal of Speech* 94, 3 (2008): 297-319.

Rasmussen, Anders Fogh. Opening Address. October 1, 2002. http://danmarkshistorien.dk/leksikon-og-kilder/vis/materiale/anders-fogh-rasmussens-v-tale-ved-folketingets-aabning-2002/?no_cache=1&cHash=6c3da8f2aa8d82c136cbcb6f4b5b2f71. Accessed January 31, 2017.

Reboul, Olivier. "The figure and the Argument." In *From Metaphysics to Rhetoric*, edited by Michel Meyer. Kluwer Academic Publishers, 1989.

Richards, I. A. *The Philosophy of Rhetoric.* London: Oxford University Press, 1936.

Ricoeur, Paul. *Fortolkningsteori*. København: Vinten, 1979.

Roer, Hanne and Marie Lund Klujeff. "Introduktion." *Rhetorica Scandinavica* vol. 57 (2011): 9-18.

Rosenberg, Rainer. "Literarischer Stil." In *Ästhetische Grundbegriffe*, vol. 5, edited by K. Barck et al. Stuttgart: Metzler, 2003: 650-644.

Rosenberg, Rainer. "Stil: Einleitung." In *Ästhetische Grundbegriffe*, vol. 5, edited by K. Barch et al. Stuttgart: Metzler, 2003: 641-650.

Samuels, Shimon. "Wiesenthal Centre's Open Letter to the People of Norway in the Oslo Daily Aftenposten, http://www.wiesenthal.com/site/apps/nlnet/content2.aspx?c=lsKWLbPJLnF&b=4442247&ct=5850849. Accessed February 5, 2017.

Schrøder, Casper Fruergaard. "Mit navn er Bono, og jeg er rockstjerne." *Retorikmagasinet* 60 (2006): 32.

Scott, Robert L. "On Viewing rhetoric as Epistemic." In *Professing the New Rhetorics. A Sourcebook*, edited by Therese Enos and Stuart C. Brown. Englewood Cliffs: Prentice Hall, 1994: 307-318.

Skyum-Nielsen, Rune. *Nr. 1. Dansk hiphopkultur siden 1983*. København: Informations forlag, 2006.

Sloane, Thomas E., ed. *Encylopedia of rhetoric*. Oxford: Oxford University Press, 2001.

Sorensen, Theodore C. *Kennedy.* London: Hodder and Stoughton, 1965.

Sorensen, Theodore C. *Counselor. A Life at the Edge of History*. New York: Harper, 2008.

Sowinski, Bernhard. *Stilistik. Stiltheorien und Stilanalysen* (2nd edition). Stuttgart: Metzler, 1999.

Sowinski, Bernhard. "Stil (lat. stilus; engl., frz. Style; ital.stile)." In *Historisches Wörterbuch der Rhetorik*, vol 8, edited by Gert Ueding. Darmstadt: Wissenschaftliche Buchgesellschaft, 2007: 1393-1419.

Swift, Jonathan. *Irish Tracts 1720-1723*, edited by Herbert Davis. Oxford, 1963.

Tate, Helen. "The Ideological Effects of a Failed Constitutive Rhetoric: The Co-option of the Rhetoric of White Lesbian Feminism." *Women's Studies in Communication* 28, 1 (2005): 1-31.

Theroux, Paul. "The Rock Star's Burden." *The New York Times*, December 15, 2005.

Thorning-Schmidt, Helle. Opening Address. October 4, 2011, http://www.stm.dk/_p_13517.html. Accessed February 6, 2017.

Ueding, G., ed. *Historisches Wörterbuch der Rhetorik*, vols 1-9. Tübingen: Max Niemeyer Verlag, 1992-2009.

Vickers, Brian. *In Defence of Rhetoric*. Oxford: Clarendon, 1988.

Villadsen, Lisa S. "Speaking on Behalf of Others." *Rhetoric Society Quarterly* 38 (2008): 25-45.

Vivian, Bradford. "Style, Rhetoric, and Postmodern Culture." *Philosophy and Rhetoric* 35, 3 (2002): 223-243.

Wagner, Uwe. "Letter to the editor." *Aftenposten*. 6 August, 2006. www.aftenposten.no/english/local/article1416800.ece.

White, Hayden. *Metahistory. The Historical Imagination in Nineteenth-Century Europe*. Baltimore: The Johns Hopkins University Press, 1973.

Willcock, Gladys Doidge and Alice Walker, eds. *The Arte of English Poesie*. Cambridge, 1936.

Wordsworth, William. *The Prose Works of William Wordsworth II*, edited by W. J. B. Owen and Jane Worthington Smyser. Oxford, 1974.

"Writing Scotland, a Journey through Scotland's Literature: Walter Scott." *BBC*. July 1, 2006. http://www.bbc.co.uk/scotland/arts/writingscotland/learning_journeys/tartan_myths/walter_scott/>. Accessed February 6, 2017.

Zagacki, Kenneth S. "Constitutive Rhetoric Reconsidered: Constitutive Paradoxes in G.W. Bush's Iraq War Speeches." *Western Journal of Communication* 71, 4 (2007): 272-293.